The Bible
BOOK
OF
LISTS

The Bible
BOOK
OF
LISTS

Joy MacKenzie
&
Shirley Bledsoe

Zondervan Publishing House
Grand Rapids, Michigan

THE BIBLE BOOK OF LISTS

Zondervan Publishing House,
1415 Lake Drive, S.E.,
Grand Rapids, Michigan

ISBN 0-310-70321-2

Printed in the United States of America

87   88   89   90 / 10   9   8   7   6

Table of Contents

PEOPLE

FAMOUS BIBLE WOMEN

Abigail
Athaliah
Bathsheba
Deborah
Delilah
Dinah
Dorcus (Tabitha)
Drusilla
Elisabeth
Esther
Eunice
Eve
Gomer
Hagar
Hannah
Herodias
Joel
Jezebel
Joanna
Jochebed
Leah

Lois
Lydia
Martha
Mary, Jesus' mother
Mary, Martha's sister
Michal
Miriam
Mary Magdalene
Naomi
Phoebe
Priscilla
Rachel
Rahab
Rebekah
Rhoda
Ruth
Salome
Sapphira
Sarah
Vashti
Zipporah

Check the "Who's Who" list to become better acquainted with these women.

JUMPIN' *GERIATRICS!!

Folks Who Lived To Be More Than 900 Years Old

Members of the "900" Club:

969—Methuselah	(Genesis 5:27)
962—Jared	(Genesis 5:20)
950—Noah	(Genesis 9:29)
930—Adam	(Genesis 5:5)
912—Seth	(Genesis 5:8)
910—Cainan	(Genesis 5:14)
905—Enos	(Genesis 5:11)

Enoch went to heaven when he was 365 years old, but he didn't die. Elijah never died, but was an old man when he was taken to heaven in a chariot of fire. These two fellows are now over 2,500 years old!!! Talk about wrinkles!

*If you don't know this word, look it up in the dictionary. It's one of the "oldest" words in the English language!"

CHRONOLOGY CONNECTION

Approximate order in history of some major Old Testament people:

Adam	Benjamin	Jehoshaphat
Eve	Aaron	Ahab
Cain	Moses	Jezebel
Abel	Miriam	Elijah
Seth	Joshua	Elisha
Enoch	Deborah	Naaman
Methuselah	Gideon	Jehu
Noah	Samson	Isaiah
Shem	Naomi	Jonah
Abraham	Ruth	Jeremiah
Sarah	Eli	Ezekiel
Rebekah	Samuel	Nehemiah
Rebekah	Saul	Nebuchadnezzar
Esau	David	Daniel
Jacob	Solomon	Shadrach,
Rachel	Jeroboam	Meshach,
Joseph	Rehoboam	Abednego

WHO CAME FIRST?

In each pair of names choose the name of the person you think came first in history and underline it. To see if you are correct, refer to the list above.

Sarah or Seth?
Noah or Naaman?
Ahab or Abel?
Rachel or Rebekah?
Daniel or Deborah?
Samson or Solomon?
Isaac or Isaiah?
Eve or Enoch?
Jezebel or Joseph?
Daniel or David?
Methuselah or Moses?
Elijah or Elisha?

Jeroboam or Rehoboam?
Jehoshaphat or Joshua?
Saul or Shem?
Adam or Aaron?
Eli or Esau?
Samuel or Solomon?
Jacob or Jehu?
Miriam or Meshach?
Benjamin or Abraham?
Jacob or Jonah?
Ezekiel or Enoch?
Jeremiah or Nehemiah?

9

HERE COME DE JUDGES!!!

The book of Judges in the Old Testament tells the story of a time in Israel's history when the people were ruled by judges. It was not a good time. The story is full of wars and bloody battles and selfish, greedy actions. Each judge did what seemed right to him rather than what God would have him do. The exception was Deborah, a woman judge who seemed determined to follow God's laws consistently. Some others started out to be good, but made wrong decisions and foolish choices.

Othniel	Judges 3:11	Jepthah	Judges 11:1-12:8
Ehud	Judges 3:15-30	Ibzan	Judges 12:8, 9
Shamgar	Judges 3:31	Elon	Judges 12:11
Deborah	Judges 4, 5	Abdon	Judges 12:15
Gideon	Judges 6, 7, 8	Samson	Judges 13-16
Tola	Judges 10:1, 2	Eli	1 Samuel 4:18
Jair	Judges 10:3-5	Samuel	1 Samuel 7:15

Look up the reference beside each judge's name and learn what mistakes each one made. Some of the stories are exciting, unusual, and even hair-raising!!!

THE TRIBES OF ISRAEL

The twelve Hebrew tribes were founded by the twelve sons of Jacob.

Reuben	Naphtali
Issachar	Gad
Dan	Judah
Simeon	Asher
Zebulun	Benjamin

Levi (sometimes not counted because their duties as priests scattered them among all the tribes)

Ephraim
Manasseh (half-tribes, children of Joseph)

PARADE OF PROPHETS

A prophet is a messenger of God. In the Old Testament, God chose prophets in several ways. Sometimes He would speak to them in a dream or vision. Often, a prophet, once called, would remain a prophet for his lifetime. Others were used by God for just one special event.

Whenever God gave a prophet a message, the prophet's job was to tell it to the people—even if he must risk his life to do so. A prophet's life was often in danger. The Hebrews believed speech had some magical power. If a prophesy came true, they thought the person who had foretold it had helped to make it happen. When prophesies were good, the prophet was a hero. But when his bad prophesies came true, he was often hated.

The most famous Old Testament prophets are:

Abraham	Micah
Moses	Jonah
Aaron	Nahum
Miriam (prophetess)	Huldah (prophetess)
Deborah (prophetess)	Zephaniah
Samuel	Jeremiah
Nathan	Habakkuk
Elijah	Daniel
Elisha	Ezekiel
Joel	Obadiah
Amos	Haggai
Hosea	Zechariah
Isaiah	Malachi

The most famous New Testament prophets are John the Baptist and Paul.

GOOD DEEDS INDEED!!

Some of the Bible's
Best Helpers

OLD TESTAMENT

1. **Aaron** and **Miriam**—helped Moses get the Israelites out of Egypt.
2. **Abigail**—gave David and his men food in spite of a selfish husband.
3. **Donkey**—spoke to Balaam to make him notice the Lord's angel.
4. **Eli**—raised Hannah's son Samuel in the tabernacle.
5. **Esther** and **Mordecai**—saved the Jews from Haman's gallows.
6. **Jonathan**—loved David and helped protect him from his father, Saul.
7. **Joseph**—interpreted dreams and warned the Egyptians to prepare for famine.
8. **Rahab**—hid Joshua's spies in Jericho.
9. **Ruth**—took care of her old and widowed mother-in-law, Naomi.
10. **Servant girl**—led Naaman to Elijah for a cure of leprosy.

NEW TESTAMENT

1. **Aquila** and **Priscilla**—took Paul in to live with them.
2. **Barnabas**—helped Paul become accepted by the believers; gave money to the needy.
3. **Dorcas**—always helped those in need.
4. **John**—took care of Mary, Jesus' mother, after the Crucifixion.
5. **Joseph**—married Mary and accepted responsibility for caring for God's Son.
6. **Lydia**—opened her home to early Christians.
7. **Martha**—busied herself with household duties when Jesus was a guest.
8. **Mary Magdalene**—brought spices for Jesus' body and then helped tell of his resurrection.
9. **Peter, James, John**—were with Jesus at special times and were considered the three disciples closest to him.
10. **Silas, Timothy, Mark**—often traveled with Paul and Barnabas on missionary journeys.

BIBLE CHILDREN

CAIN, oldest son of Adam
ABEL, son of Adam killed by Cain
SETH, third son of Adam
ISHMAEL, son of Abraham and Hagar
ISAAC, the son Abraham almost sacrificed
ESAU, hairy twin brother of Jacob
JACOB, Esau's twin who tricked his father Isaac
MIRIAM, sister of Moses
MOSES, baby boy who grew to be Israel's leader
JOSEPH, son of Jacob, sold by his brothers
BENJAMIN, Joseph's youngest brother
SAMUEL, child who served with Eli in the temple
DAVID, shepherd boy who became King of Israel
MANASSEH, 12-year-old King of Judah
JOASH, 7-year-old King of Judah
JOSIAH, 8-year-old King of Judah
DANIEL, young prisoner of Babylon who gained the king's
    favor
SHADRACH, MESHACH, ABEDNEGO, Daniel's three
    Hebrew friends
JOHN THE BAPTIST, Jesus' cousin who later baptized him
JESUS, God's Son
RHODA, the girl who left Peter standing at the gate in Acts
    12:13

Children Not Known by Name

Child fought over by two mothers—1 Kings 3:22-28
Son of the widow of Zarephath—1 Kings 17:9-15
Children, eaten by bears for laughing at Elisha—2 Kings
    2:23, 24
Shunammite's son, raised from the dead—2 Kings 4:18-37
Child boiled by his mother—2 Kings 6:29
Boy with loaves and fishes—Mark 6:30-44
Son of widow of Nain, raised from the dead—Luke 7:11-16
Jairus' daughter whom Jesus raised from the dead—
    Matthew 9:18-26

FAMOUS
BIBLE
DADS

Adam - Cain, Abel, Seth
Seth - Enos
Enoch - Methuselah
Noah - Shem, Ham, Japheth
Terah - Abraham
Abraham - Isaac, Ishmael
Isaac - Jacob, Esau
Laban - Leah, Rachel
Jacob - Gad, Asher, Joseph
   Benjamin, Dan, Naphtali,
   Reuben, Simeon, Levi,
   Judah, Issachar, Zebulun,
   Dinah
Manoah - Samson
Jesse - David
David - Absalom, Solomon
Saul - Jonathan, Michal
Jonathan - Mephibosheth
Zebedee - James, John
Zacharias - John the Baptist

14

FAMOUS BIBLE MOTHERS

Eve - Cain, Abel, Seth
Sarah - Isaac
Hagar - Ishmael
Rebekah - Jacob, Esau
Rachel - Joseph, Benjamin
Leah - Dinah, Reuben,
  Simeon, Levi, Judah,
  Issachar, Zebulun
Jochebed - Moses, Miriam,
  Aaron
Ruth - Obed
Hannah - Samuel
Bathsheba - Solomon
Jezebel - Athaliah
Elisabeth - John
Mary - Jesus
Herodias - Salome
Eunice - Timothy

15

MILITARY MASTERS

The Bible's Best-Known Soldiers

1. **Joshua** — Led the Israelites into the Promised Land
2. **Gideon** — Led 300 men against the Midianites who were thick as locusts
3. **Barak** — With Deborah, led the Israelites against Sisera
4. **Absalom** — A beloved son who led a revolt against his father, David
5. **Nebuchadnezzar** — Destroyed Jerusalem and conquered the Israelites
6. **Samson** — Killed a thousand Philistines with the jawbone of a donkey
7. **Abner** — Was commander-in-chief of Saul's army
8. **Saul** — Fought the Philistines all of his days
9. **Uriah** — Was sent to the front lines of battle to be killed because David wanted his wife, Bathsheba
10. **David** — Killed Goliath, and as Israel's greatest king, led many battles
11. **Joab** — Won many victories as the commander of David's army
12. **Naaman** — Was a great Syrian army commander whom Elisha cured of leprosy
13. **Goliath** — Was the pride of the Philistine army but was killed by young David
14. **Benaiah** — Jumped in a pit and killed a lion and later became Solomon's commander-in-chief
15. **Darius** — The Mede, conquered Babylon and made Daniel one of his presidents
16. **Jehu** — Killed Jezekel and the rest of Ahab's wicked family and was made king by Elisha
17. **Cornelius** — Was a Roman soldier whom Peter converted to Christianity

HAIRIES 'N BALDIES

There are several Bible men who were noted for being exceptionally hairy *or* for being hairless or bald. Can you read the clues below and fill in the names to complete the list?

The warrior/hunter macho-man twin brother of Jacob.

_____

Genesis 27:11-22

Never had a haircut until he met a girl named Delilah.

_____

Judges 16:17

Plucked out his own hair and beard—OUCH!!!

_____

Ezra 9:3

Had a haircut once a year, and each cut weighed two hundred shekels! (almost 5 pounds.)

_____

2 Samuel 14:26

God allowed kids who teased him and called him "Baldy" to be mauled by bears.

_____

2 Kings 2:23-25

His hair grew like eagle feathers!

_____

Daniel 4:33

Shaved his head.

_____

Job 1:20

VICIOUS VILLAINS

Satan A powerful evil force who is always against God and His people; he wages war on all that is good and is constantly working to tempt Christians to do bad things.

Abimelech Son of Gideon who killed 69 of his brothers in order to be king. *Judges 9:1-6*

Ahab Horrible, no-good king of Israel who allowed his wicked wife, Jezebel, to bring her gods into Israel. *1 Kings 16-22*

Ahaz Wicked king of Judah who let religion die; offered his own son to the idol, Moloch. *2 Kings 16, 2 Chronicles 28*

Ahaziah Son of Ahab and Jezebel and just as evil. *2 Kings 1*

Athalia Daughter of Jezebel who had her grandsons killed so she could be queen. *2 Kings 11:1-3*

Barabbas A notorious criminal freed in place of Jesus by Pilate. *Matthew 27:16*

Caiaphas High priest of Israel who planned Jesus' arrest and Crucifixion. *Matthew 26:57-68*

Delilah Tricked Samson into trusting her with his secret and then had his hair cut, allowing him to be captured and imprisoned. *Judges 16:4*

Doeg Spy for King Saul who slaughtered 85 priests who had helped David. *1 Samuel 22:18*

Goliath The Philistine giant, almost ten feet tall, killed by David with a stone from his sling. *1 Samuel 17*

Haman Plotted to kill the Jews and hang Mordecai, but thanks to Esther, ended up on the gallows himself. *Esther 9*

The Herods:

Herod the Great   Ordered the babies under two years old to be killed when the wise men told him a new king had been born. *Matthew 2:16*

Herod Antipas   Had John the Baptist imprisoned and beheaded; also judged Jesus before He was crucified. *Mark 6:17-28*

Herod Agrippa I   Persecuted the early Christians; killed James, the brother of John, and had Peter put in prison. *Acts 12*

Jezebel   Ahab's wicked queen who brought the idol Baal to Israel and considered Elijah, the prophet, her greatest enemy. *1 Kings 21*

Judas Iscariot   The apostle who betrayed Jesus with a kiss, for thirty pieces of silver. *Matthew 27:3-10*

Manasseh   Called Manasseh the Mad, a king at twelve, he was a fanatical persecutor of worshipers of God; sacrificed his own son to the idol Moloch. *2 Kings 21, 2 Chronicles 33*

Nebuchadnezzar   An "off-and-on" villain who is famous for the beautiful gardens he created in Babylon, but also for cruelty to some of God's best helpers: Daniel, Shadrach, Meshach, and Abednego. *Daniel 3*

Salome   Danced beautifully for Herod Antipas and asked for John the Baptist's head on a platter as her reward. *Matthew 14:1-12*

19

ALIVE-AGAIN GANG

Dead Folks Who Came To Life

Samuel

When Saul was threatened by the Philistines, he did not know what to do. He visited a witch and asked her to bring Samuel's body back to life so he could get his advice. What Samuel told him was not good news! *1 Samuel 28:1-25*

Son of Widow of Zarephath

Raised by Elijah *1 Kings 17:17-24*

Shunammite's Son

Raised by Elisha *2 Kings 4:18-37*

Young Man

Thrown quickly into Elisha's tomb, he came alive when his dead body touched the bones of Elisha. *2 Kings 13:21*

Saints

When Jesus died on the cross, a great earthquake took place. Tombs broke open and many holy men and women who had died were raised to life. *Matthew 27:50-54*

Son of Widow of Nain

Raised by Jesus *Luke 7:11-16*

Jairus' Daughter

Raised by Jesus *Luke 8:49-55*

Lazarus

Raised by Jesus *John 11:43, 44*

Elijah, Moses

Peter, James and John were allowed a special privilege. They got to see a little bit of Jesus' glory as Elijah and Moses reappeared from the dead to talk with Jesus at the Transfiguration. The three bodies looked white and transparent. *Mark 9:2-13*

Jesus
Hallelujah! *Matthew 28:1-10*

Dorcas of Joppa
Raised by Peter *Acts 9:36-43*

Eutychus
Fell out of a third-story window when he fell asleep during one of Paul's long sermons. Paul threw himself on the young man and put his arms around him, and he came back to life. *Acts 20:7-12*

MODELS TO MIMIC

Good Examples of Godly Behavior

GENEROSITY

Abigail—gave David food
Barnabas—sold his land to help the needy
Hannah—gave her first son to God's service
Naaman—sent gifts to Elijah
Ruth—worked in the fields to support Naomi

FRIENDLINESS

Aquila and Priscilla—welcomed believers into their home
Lydia—shared her home with early Christians
Rahab—hid Joshua's spies
Rebekah—gave water to Abraham's servant and his camels
Zacchaeus—had Jesus over for dinner

HUMILITY

Andrew—was happy for younger brother, Peter, to be "special"
John the Baptist—proclaimed Jesus the Messiah, not himself
Mary of Bethany—wiped Jesus' feet with her hair
Leah—served Jacob well though he loved her sister more
Mary—obeyed God to become the mother of the Messiah

COURAGE

Daniel—prayed
David—fought a giant
Esther—saved the Jews
Gideon—fought thousands with only 300 men
John the Baptist—spoke out against Herod

FAITH

Abraham—prepared to sacrifice an only son
Elijah—called on God to send fire
Moses—led hundreds of thousands into a wilderness
Noah—built an ark on dry land
Woman—touched Jesus' robe to make herself well

FORGIVENESS

Esau—forgave Jacob for stealing his birthright
Hosea—forgave an unfaithful wife
Jesus—forgave those who crucified Him
Joseph—forgave his brothers for selling him
Stephen—forgave those who stoned him

REPENTANCE

David—asked forgiveness for sending Uriah to war
Jonah—was sorry for not going to Nineveh
Matthew—gave up a lucrative but dishonest job
Paul—regretted persecuting Christians
Zacchaeus—gave away half his goods

REVERENCE

Ezra—instructed Jews after captivity
Mary Magdelene—followed Jesus
Samuel—heard God's voice and served Him
Solomon—built a great temple for worship
Zacharias—served as priest and raised a godly son

PATIENCE

Jacob—worked fourteen years for a wife
Job—was afflicted in every way, yet trusted God
Nehemiah—rebuilt Jerusalem's walls
Noah—survived a forty-day downpour
Sarah—had her first son at age ninety-nine

SELF-CONTROL

Balaam—refused to curse the Israelites
Daniel—spent the night in a den of lions
Joseph—recognized the brothers who sold him
A mother—offered to give up her baby so it wouldn't be divided in two
Shadrach, Meshach, Abednego—thrown into a furnace

LEADERSHIP

David—established a prosperous kingdom
Deborah—led the Israelites to a great military victory
Joshua—led his people into the Promised Land after Moses' death
Paul—established the early Christian church
Peter—was spokesman for the twelve disciples

23

ROYAL RULERS 'N ROGUES
(In Order of Appearance)

Early Old Testament Kings
Og
Balak
Abimelech
Pharaohs of Egypt

Kings of the United Kingdom of Israel
Saul
David
Solomon

Kings of the Divided Kingdom

ISRAEL	JUDAH
Jeroboam I	Rehoboam
Nadab	Abijah
Baasha	Asa*
Elah	Jehoshaphat*
Zimri	Jehoram
Tibni	Ahaziah
Omri	Athaliah
Ahab	Joash*
Ahaziah	Amaziah*
Joram	Azariah*
Jehu	Jotham*
Jehoahaz	Ahaz
Jehoash	Hezekiah*
Jeroboam II	Manesseh
Zachariah	Amon
Shallum	Josiah*
Manahem	Jehoahaz
Pekahiah	Jehoiakim
Pekah	Jehoiachin
Hoshea	Zedekiah

*This mark means that the king tried to be a good king. Most were very evil.

NOTE: Spelling of names will vary from version to version.

Roman Rulers
Caesar Augustus
Caesar Tiberias
Pilate
Felix
Festus

Babylonian Kings
Nebuchadnezzar
Belshazzar

Jewish Rulers
Herod the Great
Herod Antipas
Herod Agrippa I
Herod Agrippa II

Persian Kings
Cyrus
Darius I
Darius II

QUEENS

Rizpah—mother of seven of King Saul's sons

Michal—Saul's daughter
—David's first wife

Abigail—David's wife after her husband Nabal's death

Bathsheba—David's wife after her husband Uriah was killed
—Solomon's mother

Queen of Sheba—brought Solomon many gifts

Jezebel—just as wicked as her husband, Ahab

Athaliah—killed her grandchildren

Vashti—refused to show her beauty

Esther—saved the Jews from Haman

Belshazzar's Queen—brought Daniel to the king's attention

Herodias—asked for John the Baptist's head

Bernice—assisted her brother, King Agrippa

25

NAME'S THE SAME!!

When several people have the same name, or names that sound very much alike, it is easy to become confused as to who is who! These brief descriptions may help you "sort out" some important Bible names.

Abraham—Father of the nation of Israel
Abram—Another name for Abraham

Belshazzar—King of Babylon
Belteshazzar—Daniel's Babylonion name

Herod the Great—King of Judea when Jesus was born
Herod Antipas—Governor of Judea at Jesus' crucifixion; refused to try Jesus; had John the Baptist beheaded
Herod Agrippa—Governor of Judea who heard Paul's case
Herodias—Wife of Herod Antipas

James—One of the twelve apostles; brother of John
James—Another of the apostles; called James, the lesser
James—A brother of Jesus

Jeroboam—First king of Israel
Rehoboam—First king of Judah

John—One of the twelve apostles; brother of James
John—Another name for Mark
John the Baptist—Jesus' cousin; son of Elisabeth and Zacharias

Joseph—Son of Jacob
Joseph—Husband of Mary; Jesus' earthly father
Joseph—Brother of Jesus
Joseph of Arimathea—Buried the body of Jesus in his own new tomb

Judas—One of the twelve apostles; sometimes called Thaddeus or Lebbaeus; son of James
Judas—A brother of Jesus
Judas Iscariot—One of the twelve apostles; betrayer of Jesus

Levi—One of the twelve sons of Jacob
Levi—Another name for Matthew, the disciple

Manasseh—A son of Joseph
Manasseh—The mad king of Judah

Mary—The mother of Jesus
Mary—The sister of Martha and Lazarus
Mary Magdalene—One of Jesus' close followers; saw Jesus in the garden after the resurrection

Michael—An angel
Michal—Daughter of Saul; wife of David

Salome—Mother of James and John
Salome—Daughter of Herodias who danced for the head of John the Baptist

Saul—Name for the apostle Paul before his conversion
Saul—First king of the united kingdom

Simeon—One of Jacob's twelve sons
Simeon—A devout Christian who blessed the infant Jesus when he was dedicated at the temple.
Simon—Another name for Peter, the disciple
Simon—A brother of Jesus
Simon—A leper
Simon—A tanner
Simon—A magician
Simon of Cyrene—An early Christian who helped to carry Jesus' cross on the road to Calvary
Simon the Zealot—One of the twelve apostles

Zacharias—Father of John the Baptist
Zechariah—An Old Testament prophet
Zacchaeus—A tax collector who climbed a tree to see Jesus

(Not *persons*, but sometimes confusing...)

Ark of the Covenant—A chest which carried the stones on which the Ten Commandments were written, Aaron's rod, and a pot of manna
Noah's Ark—The boat in which Noah, his family and two or more of each animal escaped the Flood

DUPES 'N DECEPTIONS

DAVID'S WIFE, MICHAL put a statue in his bed and helped him escape through a window. *1 Samuel 19:11-14*

SOLOMON threatened to cut a baby in half in order to find the real mother. *1 Kings 3:16-28*

PAUL'S FRIENDS helped him escape over a wall at night by hiding him in a basket. *Acts 9:23-25*

REBEKAH put goatskins on Jacob's hands to trick his blind father, Isaac into believing he was his hairy brother, Esau. *Genesis 27:1-29*

HERODIAS & SALOME tricked Herod into beheading John the Baptist. *Matthew 14:6-12*

ANANIAS & SAPPHIRA sold their property and pretended to give away all their profit. *Acts 5:1-5*

DELILAH tricked Samson into telling her the secret of his strength. She had his long hair cut while he slept. *Judges 16:4-21*

LABAN tricked Jacob into marrying his older daughter, Leah, instead of the younger Rachel, whom he loved. *Genesis 29:16-28*

DAVID pretended to be a madman drooling at the mouth in order to escape his enemies. *1 Samuel 21:10-15*

MOSES' MOTHER hid him in a basket in the Nile, and after he was found and adopted by an Egyptian princess, she came to be his nurse. *Exodus 2:1-10*

THE GIBEONITES, after hearing of Joshua's conquest at Jericho, came to him in old, worn-out clothes and sandals with moldy bread to make him believe they were from a distant land. They tricked Joshua into signing a peace treaty with them which he honored even when he found out they actually lived nearby. *Joshua 9*

SAUL wished to talk to Samuel who was dead, so he sought out a witch to help him make the contact. Since he himself had banned all witches from Israel, he had to dress as a regular person so she wouldn't know he was the king. *1 Samuel 28:4-20*

To trick KING AHAB, a prophet disguised himself and pretended he was hurt. *1 Kings 20:38*

KING JEROBOAM'S WIFE disguised herself and went to the prophet Ahijah to find out if her ill son would recover. The prophet knew she was the queen as God had told him she was coming. *1 Kings 14:2*

QUEEN JEZEBEL arranged for false testimony against Naboth and had him stoned to death so King Ahab could have his vineyard! *1 Kings 21:1-13*

JOSEPH'S BOSS'S WIFE tried to get him to fall in love with her. He refused, so she lied to her husband about him and Joseph ended up in jail. *Genesis 39: 7-20*

THE CHAIN GANG
Prisoners

Joseph—Imprisoned by Potiphar whose wife falsely accused Joseph
(Genesis 39:20)

The butler and baker—Thrown into prison with Joseph
(Genesis 40:3)

Joseph's brothers—Imprisoned by Joseph, who called them spies
(Genesis 42:16)

Jeremiah—Imprisoned by King Zedekiah in a dungeon
(Jeremiah 38:6)

Jeremiah—Imprisoned by Nebuchadnezzar when he conquered Jerusalem
(Matthew 14:3-12)

John the Baptist—From prison, he sent his disciples to ask Jesus if he was the Messiah
(Matthew 11:2)

John the Baptist—Imprisoned by Herod for criticizing his marriage to Herodias
(Matthew 14:3-12)

Jesus—Betrayed by Judas and taken prisoner by the priests and elders; taken before Pilate and condemned by the people to die in place of Barabbas; heckled and made to wear a crown of thorns in prison; crucified
(Matthew 26, 27; Mark 14, 15; Luke 22, 23; John 18, 19)

Apostles—Imprisoned by the high priest, but freed by an angel
(Acts 5:17-42)

Peter—Imprisoned by Herod, but freed by an angel
(Acts 12:3-19)

Paul and Silas—Imprisoned but freed by an earthquake; their jailor was converted and baptized that same night
(*Acts 16:19-40*)

Paul—Arrested in Jerusalem; allowed to address the people and tell of his conversion; allowed a trial as a Roman citizen.
(*Acts 21-23*)

Paul—Taken to Felix; imprisoned two years during which time he appeared before Festus and Agrippa
(*Acts 24-26*)

Punishments Other Than Imprisonment

Stoning	Burning
Whipping	Loss of body parts (especially fingers and toes)
Strangling	Fetters (chains)
Blinding	Crucifixion

31

SPECIAL EVENTS IN THE LIFE
OF THE APOSTLE PAUL

1. Stephen is stoned while Saul holds the coats of the people who are throwing stones.
2. Saul is blinded and converted on the road to Damascus.
3. Saul regains his sight in Damascus. When the religious leaders try to kill him, he escapes over the city wall in a basket.
4. He works with Barnabas at the church in Antioch.
5. He begins his first missionary journey with Barnabas and John Mark.
6. His name is changed to Paul at Cyprus.
7. John Mark deserts him and Barnabas.
8. Paul and Barnabas are mistaken for gods.
9. Paul leaves on his second missionary journey with Silas. (Paul and Barnabas have separated because of a disagreement over whether to take John Mark.)
10. Timothy goes with Paul and Silas. At Troas, Paul has a vision that a man from Macedonia is begging him to go there.
11. Paul meets Lydia at Philippi, and she becomes a Christian.
12. Paul heals a girl at Philippi and is thrown into jail with Silas. An earthquake frees them, and the jailor and his family are converted.
13. He visits with Aquila and Priscilla in Corinth.
14. Paul and Silas leave on a third missionary journey.
15. Demetrius, an Ephesian silversmith, starts a riot against Paul and Silas.
16. Paul preaches at Troas where Eutychus falls asleep and tumbles from a window. Paul brings him back to life.
17. Paul visits the temple in Jerusalem where he is taken prisoner.
18. Paul's nephew discovers a plot against Paul's life, and Paul is moved to Caesarea.

19. Felix judges him at Caesarea.

20. Festus judges him at Caesarea.

21. King Agrippa judges him and is almost persuaded to become a Christian.

22. Paul sails to Rome and is shipwrecked on Malta where a poisonous snake bites him, but the bite does not kill him.

23. While still on Malta, Paul heals the governor's father.

24. Paul lives in a rented house in Rome, meeting with those who come to him for encouragement and advice.

* * *

Read 2 Corinthians 11:24-28 where Paul tells his own life story. It will make your hair stand straight on end! What a strong character Paul was!!

GOOD NEWS NETWORK

Evangelists and Missionaries

"And he said unto them, Go ye into all the world, and preach the gospel to every creature."

Mark 16:15

Men and women who obey this command of Jesus Christ are called missionaries or evangelists. They take the good news of the gospel to folks all over the world. Some of the earliest missionaries are well-known figures in the New Testament. Some of their names are listed below.

Philip	John the Baptist
Paul	The Disciples
Peter	Barnabas
Timothy	Apollos
Silas	John Mark

CHILDREN OF "SONLIGHT"

New Testament Converts

During New Testament times, becoming a follower of Christ was not a popular thing to do. Christians were usually persecuted and often murdered because of their faith. It took real courage to be a friend of Christ or even to associate with His disciples. Listed here are the names of some of those brave early Christians.

Saul (Paul)—Acts 9:3-22

Onesimus—Colossians 4:9; Philemon 10

Matthew—Matthew 9:9

Zacchaeus—Luke 19:1-10

Woman at the well—John 4:5

Priscilla and Aquila—Acts 18:26

Apollos—Acts 18:24-28

Cornelius—Acts 10

Blind beggar—John 9:35-39

Ethiopian eunuch—Acts 8:26-40

Mary Magdalene—Luke 8:2

Susanna and Joanna—Luke 8:3

Sergius Paulus, a Roman proconsul—Acts 13:7-12

Lydia—Acts 16:14, 15

Philippian jailor and his family—Acts 16:25-36

JESUS
GOD
HOLY SPIRIT

JESUS

JESUS is God in the form of a man. In this form, He is called the Son of God.

NAMES FOR JESUS...

Son of God

Son of Man

Son of Mary

Son of Joseph

The Word

Nazarene

Everlasting Father

Wonderful Counselor

Prince of Peace

Truth

Alpha and Omega

Emmanuel (Immanuel)

Rabbi

Rabboni

Christ

Mighty God

Messiah

Lily of the Valley

Rose of Sharon

The Bridegroom

Friend

The Vine

Anointed

Dayspring

Jesus of Nazareth

Man of Sorrows

My Beloved

King of Glory

King of Kings

Lord of Lords

Lord

Lord God Almighty

Lion of Judah

Holy One of God

Light

Lamb

Lamb of God

Morning Star

Good Shepherd

The Way

The Door

The Life

Master

Savior

Teacher

Judge

I Am

Daystar

35

THE GENEALOGY
OF JESUS CHRIST

The ancestry of Jesus is given in two places in the Scriptures. Matthew tells about Christ's descendants beginning with Abraham and following through each family to Joseph and Jesus. Luke writes the genealogy backwards, from Jesus all the way back to the beginning—to Adam and God. It's fun to compare the two lists. *Note:* Spelling of names will differ from version to version.

MATTHEW:

Abraham	Solomon	Shealtiel
Isaac	Rehoboam	Zerubbabel
Jacob	Abijah	Abiud
Judah	Asa	Eliakim
Perez	Jehoshaphat	Azor
Hezron	Soram	Zadok
Ram	Uzziah	Akim
Amminadab	Jotham	Eliud
Nahshon	Ahaz	Eleazar
Salmon	Hezekiah	Matthan
Boaz	Mannesseh	Jacob
Obed	Amon	Joseph
Jesse	Josiah	Jesus
David	Jeconiah	

Jesus	Elmadam	Judah
Joseph	Er	Jacob
Heli	Joshua	Isaac
Matthat	Eliezer	Abraham
Levi	Jorim	Terah
Melki	Matthat	Nahor
Jannai	Levi	Serug
Joseph	Simeon	Reu
Mattathias	Judah	Peleg
Amos	Joseph	Eber
Nahum	Jonam	Shelah
Esli	Eliakim	Cainan
Naggai	Melea	Arphaxad
Maath	Menna	Shem
Mattathias	Mattatha	Noah
Semein	Nathan	Lamech
Josech	David	Methuselah
Joda	Jesse	Enoch
Joanan	Obed	Jared
Rhesa	Boaz	Mahalaleel
Zerubbabel	Salmon	Cainan
Shealtiel	Nahshon	Enos
Neri	Amminadab	Seth
Melki	Ram	Adam
Addi	Hezron	God
Cosam	Perez	

PRAYERS OF JESUS

The Lord's Prayer . . . . *Matthew 6:9-13; Luke 11:2-4*

Thanking God for showing
  Himself to simple people . *Matthew 11:25, 26; Luke 10:21*

In the Garden of
  Gethsemane . . . . *Matthew 26:36-44; Mark 14:32-39;*
                                    Luke 23:34, 46

While on the cross . . . . *Matthew 27:46; Mark 15:34;*
                                    Luke 23:34, 46

At the raising of Lazarus . . . . . *John 11:41, 42*

Facing death . . . . *John 12:27, 28*

For His disciples . . . . *John 17*

THIRTEEN APOSTLES???

Peter
- Andrew's fisherman brother
- Leader and spokesman for the disciples
- One of three in the "inner circle" (those closest to Jesus who were with Him at special times)
- Denied Jesus three times (just as Jesus predicted)
- Believed to have been crucified upside down

James
- John's older fisherman brother and constant companion
- One of three in the "inner circle"
- First disciple killed for believing in Christ as Lord

John
- James' fisherman brother and constant companion
- One of the three in the "inner circle"
- Ambitious, angry, and often hard-hearted but became the "disciple of love" through Jesus' influence
- Asked by Jesus at the Crucifixion to care for Mary, His mother
- Outstanding leader of the early Christian church
- Wrote five books of the Bible including the Revelation
- Believed to have lived to be an old man

Andrew
- Peter's fisherman brother
- Led to Jesus by John the Baptist
- Content with his brother Peter's special relationship with Jesus
- Always bringing others to Jesus
- Thought to have been bound to a cross and left to die of hunger, thirst and exposure

Simon the Zealot
- Unknown except for his association with the Zealots, a fanatical Jewish patriot group who hated its Roman rulers
- Politically opposite of Matthew and except for the love of Jesus, probably would never have associated with him

Philip
- Not to be confused with Philip of the seven deacons
- Took his friend Nathanael (Bartholomew) to Jesus
- Asked Jesus to show the Father (God) to the disciples (Read what Jesus said in John 14:8-9.)

Thomas
- Courageously followed Jesus even when death seemed likely
- Didn't believe Jesus had come back to life until he saw the nailholes in His hands

Matthew
- Also called Levi
- Was a despised tax collector before Jesus called him
- Entertained his government friends and other sinners at a dinner where Jesus was the guest of honor (many of them were converted)

Bartholomew
- Called Nathanael in the Book of John
- Closely associated with Philip who first took him to Jesus
- Called an Israelite in whom there was no deceit

James, Son of Alpheus
- Might have been a Zealot like Simon
- Might have been Matthew's brother as they both had fathers named Alpheus, in which case, Jesus would have reconciled brothers of opposite political beliefs.

Thaddeus
- Called Judas, brother of James in Luke and Acts
- Asked Jesus why he would not show himself and all his power to the world as he had shown it to the disciples (Read what Jesus said in John 14:22-23.)

Judas Iscariot
- Probably the treasurer for the group
- Led Jesus' enemies to the Garden of Gethsemane where he betrayed Him with a kiss
- Was sorry for what he had done and gave back the thirty pieces of silver
- Hanged himself

13th! Matthias (last but not least)
- Chosen as Judas Iscariot's replacement
- Had been with the disciples from John the Baptist through the Resurrection

MIRACLES PERFORMED BY JESUS

You can read about some of Jesus' miracles in three or four different places. Matthew, Mark and Luke describe many of the same events in their books. It's fun to compare their stories and see how alike they are! The Holy Spirit sure did a super job of getting the story exactly right every time!

	MATTHEW	MARK
Changing water to wine		
Healing the nobleman's son		
Causing a huge catch of fish		
Casting out a demon		1:23-26
Healing Peter's mother-in-law	8:14, 15	1:30, 31
Healing the leper	8:1-4	1:40-42
Healing a paralyzed man	9:1-8	2:1-12
Healing a man by Bethesda Pool		
Healing a withered hand	12:9-13	3:1-5
Healing the centurion's servant	8:5-13	
Raising widow's son from dead		
Healing a demon-possessed man	12:22-37	
Calming a raging storm	8:23-27	4:37-41
Casting devils out of two men	8:28-34	5:1-15
Raising Jairus' daughter	9:18-26	5:22-24
Healing woman with a hemorrhage	9:20-22	5:23-29
Healing two blind men	9:27-31	
Casting out a demon	9:32, 33	
Feeding 5,000 people	14:15-21	6:35-44
Walking on the water	14:22-33	6:48-51
Healing Canaanite's daughter	15:21-28	7:24-30
Feeding 4,000 people	15:32-39	8:1-9
Healing a deaf-and-dumb man		7:31-37
Healing a blind man		8:22-26
Healing a mentally ill child	17:14-21	9:17-29
Causing coin to come from fish	17:24-27	
Healing ten lepers		
Healing a man born blind		
Raising Lazarus from the dead		
Healing a woman, bent double		
Healing a man with dropsy		
Causing a fig tree to wither	21:18-22	11:12-26
Healing Malchus' ear		
Causing a huge catch of fish		

40

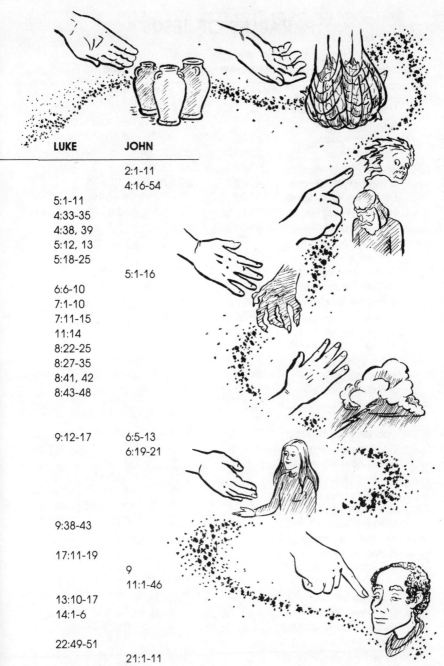

LUKE	JOHN
	2:1-11
	4:16-54
5:1-11	
4:33-35	
4:38, 39	
5:12, 13	
5:18-25	
	5:1-16
6:6-10	
7:1-10	
7:11-15	
11:14	
8:22-25	
8:27-35	
8:41, 42	
8:43-48	
9:12-17	6:5-13
	6:19-21
9:38-43	
17:11-19	
	9
	11:1-46
13:10-17	
14:1-6	
22:49-51	
	21:1-11

PARABLES OF JESUS

	Matthew	Mark	Luke
Light Under a Bushel	5:15-16	4:21-22	8:16-17
New Cloth, Old Clothes	9:16	2:21	5:36
New Wine, Old Wineskins	9:17	2:22	5:37-38
Sower of Seeds	13:3-23	4:2-20	8:4-15
Mustard Seed	13:31-32	4:30-32	13:18-19
Wicked Tenants	21:33-45	12:1-12	20:9-19
Leaves on a Fig Tree	24:32-33	13:28-29	21:29-31
House on Rock, Sand	7:24-27		6:47-49
Leaven (Yeast)	13:33		13:20-21
Lost Sheep	18:12-14		15:3-7
Talents, Pounds for			
Three Servants	25:14-30		19:11-27
Weeds in the Wheat	13:24-30		
Hidden Treasure	13:44		
Valuable Pearl	13:45-46		
Fishing Net	13:47-50		
Unmerciful Servant	18:23-35		
Workers in the Vineyard	20:1-16		
Father, Two Sons	21:28-32		
Wedding Feast	22:1-14		
Ten Bridesmaids	25:1-13		
Sheep and Goats	25:31-46		
A Growing Seed		4:26-29	
Doorkeeper on Watch		13:34-37	
Two Debtors			7:41-43
Good Samaritan			10:25-37
Friend at Midnight			11:5-10
Rich Fool			12:16-21
Ready Servants			12:37-38
Wise Manager			12:42-48
Fruitless Fig Tree			13:6-9
Place of Honor			14:7-14
Reluctant Guests			14:16-24
Lost Coin			15:8-10
Prodigal Son			15:11-32
Dishonest Manager			16:1-13
Rich Man and Lazarus			16:19-31
Servant's Duty			17:7-10
Persistent Widow			18:1-8
Pharisee and Tax Collector			18:9-14

JESUS' LAST WEEK ON EARTH

Palm Sunday
—Jesus rode into Jerusalem on a donkey.
—Crowds waved branches and shouted "Hosanna" when He passed.

Monday
—He cursed the unfruitful fig tree.
—He threw the merchants and moneychangers out of the temple.

Tuesday
—He was questioned by the authorities of the Jews.
—He named the greatest commandment.
—He told the stories of the Widow's Mite, Wicked Tenants, a Wedding Feast, Ten Bridesmaids, and the Talents.

Wednesday
—Judas conspired against Him.

Maundy Thursday
—The disciples ate the Last Supper at which Jesus washed their feet and predicted Peter's denial and Judas' betrayal.

Friday
—He prayed in the Garden of Gethsemane where Judas betrayed Him.
—He was brought before Annas, Caiaphas, the Sanhedrin, Pilate and Herod.
—He was denied three times by Peter.
—He was crucified and buried.

Saturday
—He rested in his tomb.

Sunday
—He is Risen!

Appearances After the Resurrection
—On the road to Emmaus *Luke 24:13-35*
—In Jerusalem *Luke 24:36-43, John 20:19-25*
—To the Disciples, including Thomas *John 20:26-29*
—To seven Disciples on the beach *John 21:1-23*
—To eleven Disciples on a mountain *Matthew 28:16*
—At the Ascension *Luke 24:50-53*

WHAT GOD IS LIKE

God is **REAL**.
He **ALWAYS HAS BEEN**, even before the beginning of the world.
He is **TRUTH**. He cannot lie.
He is the **CREATOR** of the whole universe. Nothing exists that was not made by Him.
He can **DO ANYTHING** He wants to do.
He **KNOWS ABSOLUTELY EVERYTHING** there is to know.
God is **EVERYWHERE** at the same time.

IN HIS VERY OWN WORDS...

The very first time God talked to a man (Moses) about Himself, this is how He described Himself:

"I am the Lord, the compassionate and gracious God,
slow to anger, abounding in love and faithfulness,
maintaining love to thousands,
forgiving wickedness, rebellion and sin.
I do not leave the guilty unpunished...
Do not worship any other god,
for the Lord whose name is Jealous, is a jealous God."
Exodus 34:5-14

OTHER DESCRIPTIONS OF GOD, BY HIMSELF...

"I am the Lord, and there is none else, there is no God beside me." *Isaiah 45:5*

"I have made the earth, the man and the beast that are upon the ground, by my great power." *Jeremiah 27:5*

"I know the things that come into your mind, every one of them." *Ezekiel 11:5*

"I have loved you with an everlasting love." *Jeremiah 31:1 NIV*

"Call upon me in the day of trouble: I will deliver thee, and thou shalt glorify me." *Psalm 50:15*

"Ye shall be holy: for I the Lord your God am holy." *Leviticus 19:2*

44

NAMES FOR GOD
USED BY
OLD TESTAMENT MEN

El (Hebrew)—"The Deity." Tells us of His divine nature.

El Shaddai—This word means "mountain." Men probably used it to describe God's strength and changelessness.

Elohim (Hebrew)—"Most supreme name." In the original language, this is a plural word, but it does NOT mean "gods." Rather, it means the ONE God who completely owns all the divine qualities.

Adon or **Adonai** (Hebrew)—"Lord" or "King." Tells us about God's divine authority and executive rule.

Yahweh (Hebrew)—"Jehovah Lord." This name comes from the Hebrew verb "to be." It means to be actively present. It tells us that God is always and forever actively present with His people. *Exodus 3:13-16*

Abba (Aramaic)—"Father" or "Daddy." It tells us of his protective, fatherly qualities and speaks about how intimately He loves His children.

Jehovah
The Holy One
The Holy One of Israel
The God "Whose Name Is
　　Jealous"
The Lord of Hosts
The True God
The Living God
The High God
The Lord Almighty
God Almighty
Creator
King
Judge
God of All Flesh
Song
Mother bird
Warrior
Dew
Redeemer
Lion
Leopard

The God of Israel
The God of the Hebrews
The Holy Redeemer
Strength of Israel
My Salvation
Rock
Help
Husband
Fountain
Light
Lamp
Shepherd
Shield
Strength
Father
Dwelling Place
Refuge
Everlasting Arms
Lord God of Hosts
Fortress
Stronghold
Bear

45

WORDS OTHERS HAVE USED TO DESCRIBE GOD...

wise in heart
mighty in strength
faithful
friend of sinners
Father
merciful
peacemaker
just
gracious
omniscient (all-knowing)
worthy
good
upright
full of lovingkindness
forgiving
perfect
omnipresent (is everywhere)
omnipotent (all-powerful)
impartial (doesn't play favorites)
longsuffering
loving
Creator
eternal (lives forever)
glorious (to be enjoyed)
holy (deserves to be worshipped)
unchangeable
infinite (has no limits—no beginning or ending)
sovereign (has supreme rank—the highest and most important office)

THE WORD FOR GOD ALMIGHTY... IN MODERN LANGUAGES

German—*Got*
French—*Dieu*
Dutch—*God*
Italian—*Dio*
Spanish—*Dios*

GOD'S ORDER OF CREATION

"In the beginning, God created the heaven and the earth."
—*Genesis 1:1*

DAY 1
God created light, day and night. *Genesis 1:1-5*

DAY 2
God separated the water to make sky and earth. *Genesis 1:6-8*

DAY 3
God gathered the water together on the earth and made dry land, hills and mountains. He made trees, plants, fruits with seeds. He also provided for reproduction. *Genesis 1:9-13*

DAY 4
God created the sun, the seasons, and the moon and stars. *Genesis 1:14-19*

DAY 5
God created sea creatures and birds. *Genesis 1:20-23*

DAY 6
God created land creatures, man and woman. *Genesis 1:24-31*

DAY 7
God rested from all his work. *Genesis 2:1-3*

"How many are your works, O Lord! In wisdom you made them all; the earth is full of your creatures."
—*Psalm 104:24 NIV*

"All things were made by him; and without him was not any thing made that was made."
—*John 1:3*

47

THE HOLY SPIRIT

WHO HE IS:

- The Holy Spirit is God living and working in the world, especially in the hearts of Christians—NOW—TODAY.
- The Holy Spirit is God's Spirit—just as Jesus is God's Son. He is part of God. He is one-third of the Trinity.
- When a person becomes a Christian, the Holy Spirit comes to live within.
- Sometimes the Holy Spirit is called the Holy Ghost—perhaps because he cannot be seen—but he is not a scary creature.

WHAT HE DOES:

1. The Holy Spirit helps Christians understand God's Word.
2. He gives them a special consciousness of what is right.
3. He helps them live as Jesus taught that His children should live.
4. He brings them courage and comfort when they are sad or afraid or troubled.
5. He produces special qualities in us if we behave and grow in a way that pleases God. The Bible calls these the "fruit of the Spirit." They are:

THE FRUITS OF THE SPIRIT

How To Tell If You Are Truly God's Person

The Bible says if you behave in a way that pleases God, then His Holy Spirit will produce in you these fruits:

Love	Goodness
Joy	Faith
Peace	Meekness
Longsuffering	Temperance
Gentleness	— *Galatians 5:22, 23*

WHAT EVERY KID SHOULD KNOW

GOD'S PLAN FOR SALVATION

If a friend should ask you, "How can I get to know God?" or "How can I become a Christian?" would you know exactly how to explain salvation?

Here is an easy ABC way of explaining God's plan for salvation.

A — Admit you are a sinner.

"All have sinned, and come short of the glory of God." *Romans 3:23*

B — Believe Jesus can and will save you from your sins.

"Believe on the Lord Jesus Christ, and thou shalt be saved." *Acts 16:31*

C — Confess to God your sin.

Talk to Him aloud. Tell Him that you believe He has died to forgive your sin. Let Him know that you want Him to be the most important thing in your life from now on.

"If thou shalt Confess with thy mouth the Lord Jesus, and shalt believe in thine heart that God hath raised him from the dead, thou shalt be saved." *Romans 10:9*

These verses are especially good ones on the topic of salvation. Look them up and read them carefully.

John 3:3	John 14:21
John 3:16, 17	Ephesians 2:8, 9
John 14:6	1 Peter 2:24

49

COMMANDMENTS

Things God Has Told Us To Do...
For Sure!!

In the Old Testament, God gave the people of Israel some special rules to help them learn how to love Him and love each other. They tell how God expects his people to act toward Him and toward others. He gave the rules to Moses at Mount Sinai. This is what God said: *

1. "You shall not put any god ahead of Me."

2. "You shall not make idols for yourselves, images of birds of the air, the animals upon the earth, or the fish and creatures of the water. You must never bow to idols or serve them, for I am a jealous God who wants your undivided love."

3. "Never speak My name in a way that will dishonor it."

4. "Keep the Sabbath day as a holy day. Six days of the week are for work, but the seventh is for rest, a Sabbath dedicated to the Lord your God."

5. "Honor your father and mother so that you will have a long life in the land I give you."

6. "You shall not murder."

7. "You shall not commit adultery."

8. "You shall not steal."
9. "You shall not witness falsely against your neighbor."

10. "You shall not desire your neighbor's belongings for your own."

In the New Testament, God gives these very important commands:

"Love the Lord your God with all your heart and with all your soul and with all your strength and with all your mind," and, "Love your neighbor as yourself!" *Luke 10:27 NIV*

"Love each other as I have loved you!" *John 15:12 NIV*

"Do to others as you would have them do to you." *Luke 6:31 NIV*

10 WAYS TO PLEASE GOD

1. **Do What God Says**—Read and study the Bible and obey His commandments.

2. **Love**—Jesus said the greatest commandment was to love God and then to love your neighbor as yourself (which may mean giving your friend the biggest piece of cake).

3. **Encourage Others**—It's easy to find another person who is in need of a "boost." A note, a special favor, or just some kind words could help someone else through a difficult situation.

4. **Share**—Give of yourself, your time and your talents as well as your possessions.

5. **Forgive Others**—Remember God will forgive you in the same way that you forgive others. You should try hard not to hold grudges when others mistreat you. Forgive and forget!

6. **Go to Church**—Church is an opportunity to be with other believers and to show God you love Him. Imagine having to explain to Him one day why you didn't visit His house. Ugh!

7. **Pray**—Talk to God every day—thanking Him, praising Him, and telling Him your problems—then listening to Him talk to you.

8. **Take Care of Your Body**—You've heard it before: exercise, avoid junk food, get plenty of rest, take only prescribed medicines. It will make you feel enthusiastic about living, which is exactly the way God wants you to feel.

9. **Set a Good Example**—God wants you to influence others for Him. The best way to do that is to live so that His influence shows in your own life.

10. **Be Joyful**—One of God's promises is that if you invite His Holy Spirit into your heart, you will receive joy.

*as written in *The Book of Life* by
Dr. V. Gilbert Beers, Zondervan. Used by permission.

DRESS FOR SUCCESS
The Armor of God

In Ephesians 6:10-17, we are told what to wear to protect us from the Devil.

1. Buckle the **BELT OF TRUTH** around your waist.

   Always tell the truth, admire others who are honest, and remember that God never lies.
   Read Psalm 100:5.

2. Strap the **BREASTPLATE OF RIGHTEOUSNESS** on your chest.

   Protect your heart by not letting harmful feelings in or out. Do not mistreat other people, and when others hurt you, forgive them and then forget about it.
   Read Isaiah 54:14.

3. Fit your feet with the **GOSPEL OF PEACE**.

   The Bible says the Lord hates feet that are fast in running to mischief. Being kind and considerate of others will help you find the path to feeling content and happy.
   Read Proverbs 2:20.

4. Take up the **SHIELD OF FAITH**.

   Trust God to take care of you. Don't worry about what might happen, for God promises us He will help us get through anything.
   Read Psalm 56:11.

5. Wear the **HELMET OF SALVATION** on your head.

   Use your brain and learn about Jesus. Believe that He is God, that He came back to life after being crucified, and that when you die you will go to heaven.
   Read Romans 10:9.

6. Grasp the **SWORD OF THE SPIRIT** in your hand.

Read and study the Bible to learn about God's
Spirit. The Bible is the Word of God and is a mighty
weapon against evil.

Read Hebrews 4:1.

WORDS TO LIVE BY

40 Of The Bible's Most Quoted Scriptures

"Thou shalt love the Lord thy God with all thy heart, and with all thy soul, and with all thy mind." *Matthew 22:37*

"In everything, do to others what you would have them do to you." *Matthew 7:12 NIV*

"Trust in the Lord with all thine heart; and lean not unto thine own understanding." *Proverbs 3:5*

"For all have sinned, and come short of the glory of God." *Romans 3:23*

"Believe on the Lord Jesus Christ, and thou shalt be saved, and thy house." *Acts 16:31*

"Do not boast about tomorrow, for you do not know what a day may bring forth." *Proverbs 27:1 NIV*

"So then every one of us shall give account of himself to God." *Romans 14:12*

"Casting all your care upon him; for he careth for you." *1 Peter 5:7*

"For the wages of sin is death; but the gift of God is eternal life through Jesus Christ our Lord." *Romans 6:23*

"Children, obey your parents in the Lord: for this is right." *Ephesians 6:1*

"Let no man despise thy youth; but be thou an example of the believers..." *1 Timothy 4:12*

"The fool says in his heart, There is no God." *Psalm 14:1 NIV*

"Without faith it is impossible to please God." *Hebrews 11:6 NIV*

"Now faith is being sure of what we hope for and certain of what we do not see." *Hebrews 11:1 NIV*

"I am the way, the truth and the life: no man cometh unto the Father, but by me." *John 14:6*

"There is one God, and one mediator between God and men, the man Christ Jesus." *1 Timothy 2:5*

"Love thy neighbor as thyself." *Matthew 22:39*

"Be ye doers of the word, and not hearers only." *James 1:22*

"All scripture is given by inspiration of God." *2 Timothy 3:16*

"A friend loveth at all times." *Proverbs 17:17*

"A soft answer turneth away wrath." *Proverbs 15:1*

"Be ye kind one to another, tenderhearted, forgiving one another." *Ephesians 4:32*

"Forgive, and ye shall be forgiven." *Luke 6:37*

"All things were made by him; and without him was not anything made that was made." *John 1:3*

"God is our refuge and strength, a very present help in trouble." *Psalm 46:1*

"Even a child is known by his doings, whether his work be pure, and whether it be right." *Proverbs 20:11*

"The Lord is my shepherd; I shall not want." *Psalm 23:1*

"The grass withers and the flowers fall, but the word of our God stands forever." *Isaiah 40:8 NIV*

"The prayer of a righteous man is powerful and effective." *James 5:16 NIV*

"If we confess our sins, he is faithful and just to forgive us our sins, and to cleanse us from all unrighteousness." *1 John 1:9*

"If anyone acknowledges that Jesus is the Son of God, God lives in him and he in God." *1 John 4:15 NIV*

"For God so loved the world, that he gave his only begotten Son, that whosoever believeth in him should not perish, but have everlasting life." *John 3:16*

"Except a man be born again, he cannot see the kingdom of God." *John 3:3*

"Jesus Christ is the same yesterday and today and forever." *Hebrews 13:8 NIV*

"It is more blessed to give than to receive." *Acts 20:35*

"Whatsoever a man soweth, that shall he also reap." *Galatians 6:7*

"In the beginning, God created the heaven and the earth." *Genesis 1:1*

"Create in me a clean heart, O God; and renew a right spirit within me." *Psalm 51:10*

"For where two or three come together in my name, there am I with them." *Matthew 18:20 NIV*

"Thou wilt keep him in perfect peace, whose mind is stayed on thee: because he trusteth in thee." *Isaiah 26:3*

WHERE TO FIND IT... FAST!

Armor of God	Ephesians 6:10-17	
Ascension	Mark 16:19	Luke 24:50, 51
Beatitudes	Matthew 5:3-12	
Disciples		
call of	Matthew 4:18-19	Mark 1:16-17
the 12 named	Matthew 10:2-4	Mark 3:16-19
Creation	Genesis 1 & 2	
Crucifixion	Matthew 27:33-44	Mark 15:22-32
Flood	Genesis 7	
Fruits of the Spirit	Galatians 5:22, 23	
Golden Rule	Matthew 7:12	Luke 6:31
Great Commandment	Matthew 22:34-40	Mark 12:28-34
Great Commission	Matthew 28:19-20	Mark 16:15
Jesus' Life and Ministry	Matthew	Mark
birth	Matthew 1 & 2	Luke 2:1-20
boy/temple	Luke 2:41-52	
baptism	Matthew 3:13-17	Mark 1:9-11
Last Supper	Matthew 26:17-29	Mark 14:13-25
Little Gospel	John 3:16-17	
Lord's Prayer	Matthew 6:9-13	Luke 11:2-4
Love Chapter	1 Corinthians 13	
* Parables:		
Good Samaritan	Luke 10:29-37	
Lost sheep	Matthew 18:12-14	Luke 15:3-7
Prodigal son	Luke 15:11-32	
Sower	Matthew 13:3-23	Mark 4:2-20
Pentecost	Acts 2:1	
Plagues	Exodus 7-12	
Resurrection	Matthew 28	Mark 16
Psalm of Thanksgiving	Psalm 100	Psalm 103:1-6
Sermon on the Mount	Matthew 5-7	
Shepherd Psalm	Psalm 23	
Ten Commandments	Exodus 20:1-17	Deuteronomy 5:6-21
Transfiguration	Matthew 17:1-13	Mark 9:2-13

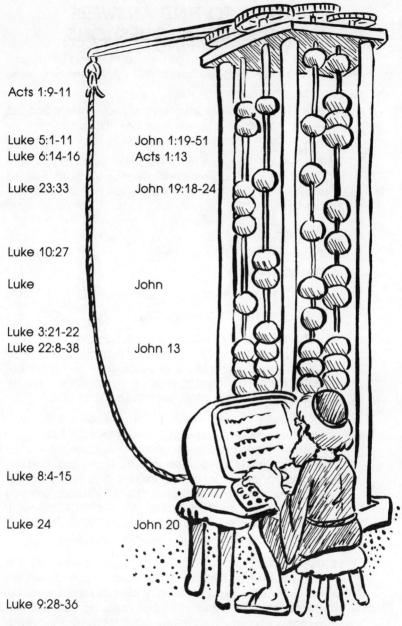

Acts 1:9-11

Luke 5:1-11   John 1:19-51
Luke 6:14-16   Acts 1:13

Luke 23:33   John 19:18-24

Luke 10:27

Luke   John

Luke 3:21-22
Luke 22:8-38   John 13

Luke 8:4-15

Luke 24   John 20

Luke 9:28-36

* See a complete listing of parables elsewhere in this book.

HOW TO FIND ANSWERS
TO SPIRITUAL QUESTIONS

1. READ GOD'S WORD—to get His opinion on the subject! (Some other suggestions in this list will tell you more about how to do that.)

2. PRAY—that the Holy Spirit will help you understand the real truth about answers that are difficult to find. (It works! Much of the Bible was written by this very process!)

3. THINK—Use the good mind God has given you to try to figure out a fair, logical answer that would be in keeping with God's laws and good Christian standards of behavior.

4. ASK YOUR PARENTS

5. ASK YOUR CHRISTIAN FRIENDS

6. ASK YOUR PASTOR

7. ASK YOUR SUNDAY SCHOOL TEACHER

8. ASK YOUR DEACONS OR ELDERS

9. USE A BIBLE DICTIONARY—Bible dictionaries are organized like all other dictionaries—in ABC order, but they tell more than just definitions of words. They give short, but quite complete descriptions of many Bible persons, places, and things, often with illustrations.

10. USE A BIBLE CONCORDANCE—A complete Bible concordance is usually a huge, fat book that contains every word written in the Bible. So if you know only ONE word in a particular verse, you can look up that word, and the concordance will give a reference and quote part of each verse in the Bible that contains that word. To use a concordance, try to identify the KEY WORD in your question. Locate that word in the concordance (in ABC order) to find all the Scriptures that use that word.

11. USE A BIBLE COMMENTARY—Bible commentaries are books written by Bible scholars, explaining each verse of each chapter, word by word or idea by idea. Of course, the authors give their own particular opinion or interpretation, usually in scholarly, adult language. But reading a commentary on a certain verse or passage will help you discover ideas you may not have considered by yourself.

12. USE A BIBLE ATLAS—A book of maps related to Bible times.

13. VISIT YOUR CHURCH LIBRARY—Ask the librarian.

14. VISIT A CHRISTIAN BOOKSTORE—Ask about books and materials on the subject you want to explore.

15. WRITE OR CALL GRANDMA AND GRANDPA—(Maybe you should do this first!)

HARD QUESTIONS TO ANSWER
(Ones That Smart Kids Often Ask)

1. Why are we supposed to fear God? Does He want us to be afraid of Him?

2. Is the Holy Ghost anything like Casper? Why is He called a ghost?

3. Why does God let bad things happen to good people, especially to innocent children?

4. What happens to a person the minute he dies?

5. Does God talk to kids nowadays? Exactly how does He do that?

6. Are angels real? Do people really have guardian angels?

7. Are fortune-tellers bad? Is it a sin to have your fortune told?

8. Is there a difference between "God," "Jesus," and "the Lord"?

9. How can God be God and still be Jesus and the Holy Spirit at the same time?

10. How can God know and take care of all the people and things in the world at the same time?

11. The Bible says if you ask anything in Jesus' name, God will do it. Then why do we sometimes not get what we ask for?

12. How does a kid get to know God?

13. Does a person have to be baptized to get to heaven? What is baptism for?

14. Will God still love me if I disobey His commands?

MONSTERS THAT GET KIDS...

'Ya Better Watch Out!

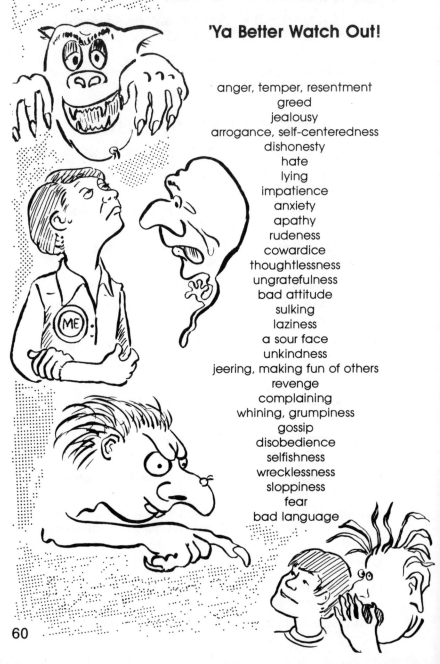

anger, temper, resentment
greed
jealousy
arrogance, self-centeredness
dishonesty
hate
lying
impatience
anxiety
apathy
rudeness
cowardice
thoughtlessness
ungratefulness
bad attitude
sulking
laziness
a sour face
unkindness
jeering, making fun of others
revenge
complaining
whining, grumpiness
gossip
disobedience
selfishness
wrecklessness
sloppiness
fear
bad language

MONSTER MASHERS

Go get 'um!!

truthfulness
honesty
obedience
purity
wisdom
thankfulness
forgiveness
generosity
gentleness
willingness to work
friendliness
reasonableness
confidence in God
courage
reverence
dependability
a thankful heart
sensitivity
peace
kindness
a cheerful spirit
humility
caring
honor
patriotism
a healthy mind and body
patience
faith
hope
love

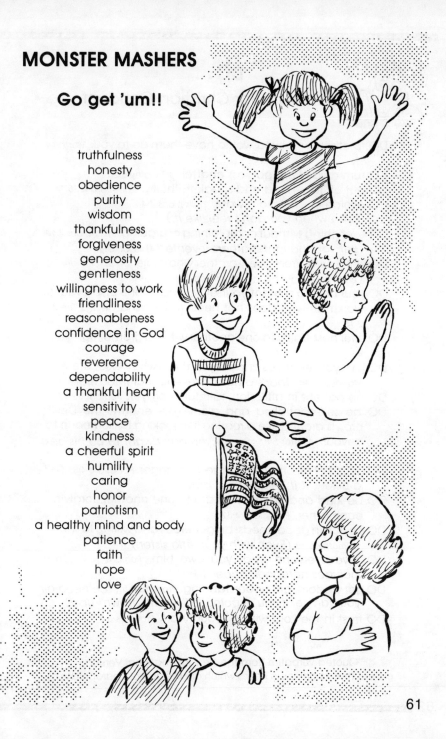

61

DO...
Prescription for Christian Conduct

DO to others what you would have them do to you. *Matthew 7:12*

DO turn away from godless chatter. *1 Timothy 6:20*

DO put off falsehood and speak truthfully. *Ephesians 4:25*

DO rejoice in the Lord always. *Philippians 4:4*
(*Even when you don't feel like it.*)

DO everything without complaining or arguing. *Philippians 2:14*
(*Bet you thought mothers invented this one!*)

DO keep away from every brother who is idle. *2 Thessalonians 3:6*
(*Laziness can be contagious.*)

DO your best to present yourself to God as one approved, a workman who does not need to be ashamed. *2 Timothy 2:15*

DO offer hospitality to one another without grumbling. *1 Peter 4:9*

DO love your enemies and pray for those who persecute you. *Matthew 5:44* (*That's a hard one—but not impossible!*)

DO be patient in affliction, faithful in prayer. *Romans 12:12*

DO be self-controlled and alert. Your enemy, the Devil, prowls around like a roaring lion looking for someone to devour. *1 Peter 5:8* (*Surely you don't want to be his next meal!*)

DO get rid of all bitterness, rage, and anger. *Ephesians 4:31* (*Hit a pillow, if it helps—then pray!*)

DO be kind and compassionate to one another, forgiving each other. *Ephesians 4:32*

DO be rich in good deeds; be generous and willing to share. *1 Timothy 6:18* (*Even with your little sister.*)

DO give everyone what you owe him. *Romans 13:7* (*That includes notebook paper!*)

DO get wisdom, get understanding. *Proverbs 4:5* (*You need all you can get if you're going to live with grown-ups!*)

DO trust in the Lord with all your heart. *Proverbs 3:5*

"Quoted verbatim from the New International Version,
except those portions in italics which are the author's paraphrase."

DO NOT...

DO NOT be anxious about anything... present your requests
to God. *Philippians 4:6*

DO NOT tire of doing what is right. *2 Thessalonians 3:13*

DO NOT have anything to do with foolish and stupid argu-
ments. *2 Timothy 2:23*

DO NOT be overcome by evil, but overcome evil with good.
Romans 12:21

DO NOT repay anyone evil for evil. *Romans 12:17*

DO NOT be proud, but be willing to associate with people of
low positions; do not be conceited. *Romans 12:16*

DO NOT put your hope in wealth. *1 Timothy 6:17*

DO NOT let any unwholesome talk come out of your mouths.
Ephesians 4:29 (Unkind words are dirty too!)

DO NOT let the sun go down while you are still angry. *Ephesians
4:26*

DO NOT get drunk on wine. *Ephesians 5:18*
(Or anything!!)

DO NOT withhold good from those who deserve it. *Proverbs 3:27*

DO NOT love sleep or you will grow poor. *Proverbs 20:13 (God
hates laziness.)*

DO NOT withhold discipline from a child. *Proverbs 23:13 (Hope
Dad doesn't read this one!)*

DO NOT be quick with your mouth. *Ecclesiastes 5:2 (You might
put your foot in it.)*

DO NOT pass judgment on one another. *Romans 14:13*

DO NOT seek your own good but seek the good of others.
1 Corinthians 10:24

DO NOT be misled: "Bad company corrupts good character." *1 Corinthians 15:33*

DO NOT forsake your friend. *Proverbs 27:10*

DO NOT be carried away by all kinds of strange teachings.
Hebrews 13:9

DO NOT be ashamed to testify about our Lord. *2 Timothy 1:8*

DO NOT merely listen to the Word. Do what it says. *James 1:22*

DO NOT boast about tomorrow, for you do not know what a
day may bring forth. *Proverbs 27:1*

"Quoted verbatim from the New International Version,
except those portions in italics which are the author's paraphrase."

EIGHT THINGS
WORTH THINKING ABOUT

Do you like to daydream... or just think great thoughts and let your mind play with super ideas? God's Word tells us that our thought time can be best spent on some of the things in this list. The original list is found in Philippians 4:8.

THINK ABOUT THINGS THAT ARE:

TRUE (sure, reliable, real, trustworthy)

_____

HONEST (noble, genuine, sincere)

_____

RIGHT (just, blameless, fair, honorable)

_____

PURE (innocent, faultless, clean)

_____

LOVELY (perfect, flawless, radiant, beautiful)

_____

ADMIRABLE (edifying, of good report or character)

_____

EXCELLENT (virtuous, moral, righteous)

_____

PRAISEWORTHY (exemplary, things of wonderful quality)

_____

Under each item in the list, you might like to write one real thing related to that idea which you could enjoy thinking about. Look up in a dictionary the words you don't know. They are all good words to understand.

There is one special person who is all of these things.
If you know His name, write it here.

_____

HOW TO BE HAPPY

The Beatitudes*—Matthew 5

The word *beatitude* means supreme blessedness or happiness. One day Jesus left the crowds that followed Him and took just His disciples and special friends up into a mountain where He taught them how to be happy.

Happy are those who are humble,
  for God will share His home with them.

Happy are those who express their sorrow,
  for God will bring His comfort to them.

Happy are those who do not demand much,
  for God will give them the world.

Happy are those who desire to please Him,
  for God will give them a satisfied heart.

Happy are those who show mercy to others,
  for God will reward them with His own.

Happy are those whose hearts are pure,
  for God will be their friend.

Happy are those who lead others to peace,
  for God will claim them as His own children.

Happy are those who are treated wrongfully because
  they do what God desires,
  for God will give them heaven for their reward.

Happy are you when others insult you and persecute you
  and say evil against you because you are Mine.

Be glad! Be very glad!
  for God will reward you greatly in heaven,
  for even the prophets were treated this way.

*as written in *The Book of Life* by
Dr. V. Gilbert Beers, Zondervan. Used by permission.

SYMBOLS
OF THE
CHRISTIAN FAITH

Apple—Temptation; Sin

Butterfly—Easter; Resurrection; New Life

Candle—Light; Jesus, the Light of the World

Circles (Trefoil)—The Trinity (God the Father, Son and Holy Spirit); God's Love; Salvation

Crown—Christ the King

Crown of Thorns—Sufferings of Christ

Dove (Descending)—The Holy Spirit **(With Olive Branch)**—Peace, Forgiveness

Eye—God the Father who knows all, sees all things

Fire, Flames—Presence of God

Fish—Salvation; Secret symbol of early Christians

Heart—Love

Lamb—Christ, the Lamb of God

Lily—Easter; Resurrection

Menorah—Old Testament

Palm Branches—Palm Sunday;
 Victory

Rainbow—God's promise not to flood
 the entire earth again

Staff—The Good Shepherd, Jesus

Star (5 Points)—Star of Bethlehem—
 Jesus' Birth
 (6 Points)—Star of David—
 Judaism and now the modern
 country of Israel

Sun—Jesus, Son of Righteousness

Sword—The Spirit, conqueror of evil

Tablets—Ten Commandments

Tree—Tree of Life; Jesus said, "I am
 the vine."

Triangles—The Trinity (God the
 Father, Son and Holy Spirit)

67

FAMOUS PRAYERS OF THE BIBLE

Abraham's prayer for Sodom—*Genesis 18:22-23*

Moses' thanksgiving prayer for deliverance from Egypt—*Exodus 15*

Moses' intercession for Israel after they had worshipped the golden calf—*Exodus 32*

Joshua's prayer for time to win an important battle—The sun stood still!—*Joshua 10*

Gideon's prayer for signs—*Judges 6*

Hannah's prayer for a son—*1 Samuel 1*

Hannah's thanksgiving prayer—*1 Samuel 2*

Solomon's prayer for wisdom—*1 Kings 3*

Elijah's prayer to prove his God to the prophets of Baal—*1 Kings 18*

David's prayer for Solomon—*1 Chronicles 29*

Nehemiah's prayer for his people—*Nehemiah 1*

Job pleads with God—*Job 13, 14*

Job's confession—*Job 42*

The Psalms—Many prayers of petition, confession and thanksgiving

Hezekiah's prayer for his life—The sundial moved back 10 degrees!—*Isaiah 38*

Daniel's prayer about the king's dream—*Daniel 2*

The Lord's Prayer—*Matthew 6:9-13; Luke 11:2-4*

Christ's prayer in the Garden of Gethsemane—*Mark 14:32-39*

Christ's prayer on the cross—*Matthew 27:46*

Christ's prayer for His disciples—*John 17*

Mary's thanksgiving prayer—*Luke 1:46-55*

Zechariah's prayer—*Luke 1:68-79*

Stephen's prayer at his death—*Acts 7:59-60*

PRAYERS TO QUOTE

"O Lord, our Lord, how excellent is thy name in all the earth!"
Psalm 8:9

"I will praise thee, O Lord, with my whole heart; I will shew forth all thy marvelous works."
Psalm 9:1

"Create in me a clean heart, O God; and renew a right spirit within me."

Psalm 51:10

"Search me, O God, and know my heart: try me, and know my thoughts: And see if there be any wicked way in me, and lead me in the way everlasting."

Psalm 139:23

"Praise ye the Lord. O give thanks unto the Lord; for he is good: for his mercy endureth forever."

Psalm 106:1

"Thou art worthy, O Lord, to receive glory and honour and power: for thou hast created all things, and for thy pleasure they are and were created."

Revelation 4:11

THE LORD'S PRAYER

Matthew 6:9-13

"Our Father which art in heaven, Hallowed be thy name.
Thy kingdom come. Thy will be done in earth, as it is in heaven.
Give us this day our daily bread.
And forgive us our debts, as we forgive our debtors.
And lead us not into temptation, but deliver us from evil:
For thine is the kingdom, and the power, and the glory, for ever. Amen."

—from the King James translation

"Our Father in heaven:
Your name is honored,
Your kingdom is welcome.
Let Your will be done here on earth
As it is done in heaven.
Give us today the food that we need,
And forgive our sins against You,
As we forgive the sins of others against us.
Lead us not into difficult times of testing,
But keep us safe from the Evil One."

—as written in *The Book of Life*
by Dr. V. Gilbert Beers, Zondervan.
Used by permission.

WHAT TO DO WHEN YOU PRAY

Praying is having conversation with God.

1. Think of prayer time as a time when you sit down in a quiet place to talk things over with God... just as you would have a serious, quiet conversation with a best friend.

2. Use your regular voice and regular words.

3. Remember that God already knows everything about you and understands every detail about your life. He just wants you to talk to Him about it. Share your feelings and thoughts with Him.

4. First, call His name. Address Him, just as you start a conversation with your mother by saying, "Mom, I...", start by saying, "Father..."

5. Next, tell God what you think about Him. Thank Him for being your friend. Compliment Him on His wonderful work. Tell Him all the things you are happy about.

6. Then tell Him the things you are worried or concerned about. Share your needs and ask Him to help you solve special problems.

7. Ask Him for special favors for others. (Remember, He cares about brothers and friends, sisters and cousins, presidents and mayors, parents and teachers, even cats and dogs and hamsters and toads!)

8. Last of all, thank Him for all the things you can think of that are important to you... and for the answers to your prayer that He is already working on!

9. Before you finish your conversation, be sure to give God some time to talk to you. Prayer isn't just our talking to God. We need to listen too. Be quiet with God, and let Him put His thoughts and feelings in your mind. That is the way He answers our prayers sometimes!

10. Then close your prayer by saying, "In Jesus' name..." because it is through Jesus, God's Son, that we can come to God.

11. Don't forget that you can talk to God ANYTIME, ANY-WHERE, about ANYTHING. He is your very best friend in the world.

P.S.: Just in case you ever wonder whether God can really hear and answer prayer, read the story about Elijah's far-out prayer in 1 Kings 18. God's answer was fantastic!!!

WHAT TO DO
WHEN YOU HAVE SINNED

"If we confess our sins, he is faithful and
just to forgive us our sins, and to cleanse
us from all unrighteousness."
1 John 1:9

1. ADMIT TO YOURSELF THAT WHAT YOU HAVE DONE IS REALLY SIN—not just a mistake—not something you **had** to do for some reason—not something someone else **made** you do. It is good to say it aloud to yourself. Make no excuses.

2. TELL GOD WHAT YOU HAVE DONE. Of course, He already knows, but He wants to hear you say it.

3. ASK HIM TO FORGIVE YOU. If you have hurt someone else with this sin, ask Him to help you make it right with them.

4. GO TO ANY OTHER PERSON OR PERSONS YOU HAVE HURT BY YOUR SIN. Tell them God has forgiven you and you would like to ask their forgiveness too.

5. THANK GOD FOR HIS FORGIVENESS. Tell Him you love Him. The more we praise Him and the better we get to know Him, the less likely we are to sin.

"Your sins are washed away, and you are
set apart for God, and he has accepted
you because of what the Lord Jesus
Christ and the Spirit of our God have
done for you."
1 Corinthians 6:11 LB

WHAT TO DO WHEN YOU WORSHIP

Worship is saying to God in every way you can think of, "God, you are wonderful... You are terrific... You are super... and I love you!"

1. God is good at everything: Think of at least three things He's good at doing. Tell Him about each one and compliment Him on his good work.

2. For each category below, name one specific thing that God has made:

   mammal _____

   plant _____

   human _____

   fish _____

   bird _____

   water _____

   sky _____

   land _____

   Read your list aloud to God. Tell Him how happy you are that He made each one.

3. Look at something in your world that is particularly beautiful. Clap your hands in praise to show God your excitement!

4. Picture in your mind the scene at the crucifixion... Christ hanging on the cross. Try to feel how He must have felt... how His body hurt and His heart was broken... How embarrassed He must have been to be hanging up there in front of the world like a criminal, deserted by all His friends, even by His own Father. Tell Him how much you love Him for going through that awful experience so that you could be His child and have eternal life in heaven.

5. Use one of these songs or another of your own choosing to express joyfully your love and praise to God. Sing it with loud excitement.

72

"Praise Him, Praise Him"
"Praise God From Whom All Blessings Flow"
"I Just Came To Praise The Lord"
"Hallelu, Hallelu"
"Praise Ye the Lord, the Almighty"

6. Read these Scriptures aloud to God with great enthusiasm:

Psalm 150   Psalm 104
Psalm 139   Psalm 105:1-3
Psalm 100   Psalm 106:1-3
Psalm 103

7. Find a quiet, peaceful place where you can be alone and just "be with Him"... Be quiet with Him as you would be with a close friend. Doesn't it feel good to be friends with God?

GOOD THINGS TO MEMORIZE FROM GOD'S WORD

- The Books of the Bible
- The Ten Commandments—*Exodus 20:3-17*
- The Beatitudes—*Matthew 5:3-12*
- The Lord's Prayer—*Matthew 6:9-13*
- The Great Commandment—*Luke 10:27*
- The Golden Rule—*Luke 6:31*
- The Shepherd's Psalm—*Psalm 23*
- The Thanksgiving Psalm—*Psalm 100*
- The Love Chapter—*1 Corinthians 13*
- The Little Gospel—*John 3:16, 17*
- The Fruits of the Spirit—*Galatians 5:22*

BOOKS OF THE BIBLE

OLD TESTAMENT (39 Books)

BOOK	CONTENT	FAMOUS CHARACTERS
Genesis	Creation; the Flood; the stories of the patriarchs; Joseph in Egypt.	Adam, Eve, Noah, Abraham, Sarah, Isaac, Rebekah, Esau, Jacob, Rachel, Joseph
Exodus	Slavery in Egypt; the ten plagues; Passover; exit from Egypt; the Ten Commandments.	Moses, Aaron, Miriam
Leviticus	Rules for priests, worship, festivals, tithes, and godly behavior.	Moses, Aaron
Numbers	The counting and organization of the Israelites by Moses; 40 years in the wilderness; laws for the Israelites; appointment of Joshua.	Moses, Aaron, Miriam, Joshua, Caleb, Balaam
Deuteronomy	Moses' sermons; repetition of the Ten Commandments; sighting of the Promised Land; Moses' death; appointment of Joshua.	Moses, Joshua
Joshua	Fall of Jericho; conquest of the Promised Land; Joshua's death.	Joshua, Caleb, Rahab, Achan

Book	Description	Key Figures
Judges	Strengthening of Israel's rule over Canaan under the leadership of the "judges."	Deborah, Barak, Gideon, Abimelech, Jephthah, Samson
Ruth	Story of King David's great-grandmother who showed it was possible to live according to the will of God even in times of crisis.	Ruth, Naomi, Boaz
1 Samuel	Samuel's life; rise and fall of King Saul; secret anointment of David.	Hannah, Eli, Samuel, Saul, David, Jonathan, Goliath, Nabal, Abigail
2 Samuel	Saul's death; David's reign.	David, Saul, Jonathan, Ish-bosheth, Mephibosheth, Bathsheba, Absalom, Joab
1 Kings	David's death; Solomon's reign; division of the kingdom; conflict between Elijah and Ahab.	Solomon, Queen of Sheba, Ahijah, Rehoboam, Jeroboam, Ahab, Jezebel, Elijah, Elisha
2 Kings	Elijah and Elisha's ministries; rule of kings of Israel and Judah until the fall to the Babylonians.	Elijah, Elisha, Ahaziah, Naaman, Jehu, Hezekiah, Isaiah, Manasseh, Josiah
1 Chronicles	Genealogy of David; Saul's death; reign of David; David's first psalm of thanksgiving.	David, Saul, Solomon

BOOK	CONTENT	FAMOUS CHARACTERS
2 Chronicles	Glory of Solomon's reign; rule of the kings until the destruction of Jerusalem and exile of the people of Babylon.	Solomon, Hezekiah
Ezra	Return to Jerusalem after Babylonian captivity; rebuilding of the Temple; ministry of Ezra.	Ezra, Haggai, Zechariah
Nehemiah	Continuing story of restored life in Jerusalem; rebuilding of the walls; Nehemiah's ministry warning people not to repeat the sins of the past.	Nehemiah
Esther	Story of a brave queen's successful attempt to save the Jews' lives.	Esther; Ahasuerus; Haman; Mordecai
Job	Job's loss of health and wealth; his restoration to prosperity because of his unfailing trust in the Lord.	Job
Psalms	Songs of sorrow, happiness, anger, doubt, faith, repentance, praise.	
Proverbs	Instructions for good living; advice to children and parents about discipline, justice, talk, money, wisdom, morals, behavior.	

Book	Summary	Key People
Ecclesiastes	A look at the uselessness of living to please oneself rather than fearing God and keeping His commandments.	Solomon
Song of Solomon	Songs about love.	Isaiah, Hezekiah
Isaiah	Prophecies about the future of Judah and Israel, God's judgment of sin, and the coming Messiah; a message of salvation.	
Jeremiah	Call for repentance to the people living in the last 40 years of Judah's existence; prophecies about the captivity, restoration through God, and God's judgment on the foreign nations.	Jeremiah
Lamentations	A funeral song for Jerusalem after its fall to the Babylonians.	
Ezekiel	A message warning of the fall of Jerusalem, but followed by a message of hope for the future because of God's faith in His people.	Ezekiel
Daniel	Daniel's captivity in Babylon; the fiery furnace; prophecies of world empires to come and the Messiah's arrival.	Daniel, Shadrach, Meshach, Abednego, Nebuchadnezzar, Darius
Hosea	Love story about Hosea and his unfaithful wife, Gomer—symbolic of God's love for His people; prophesy of Israel's fall and punishment; promise of mercy.	Hosea, Gomer

BOOK	CONTENT	FAMOUS CHARACTERS
Joel	A call to the people of Jerusalem to repent; plague of locusts; promise of a bright future.	
Amos	A fiery message that God demands righteousness of His people.	
Obadiah	A prophecy against Edom, a nation helpful in bringing about the fall of Jerusalem; a promise of Judah's restoration.	
Jonah	Story of Jonah's flight from God but of his final success in carrying God's message to the Assyrians.	
Micah	Message to the capital cities of Judah and Israel criticizing their arrogance, pride, and lack of concern for the poor people; prophecy of the coming of Christ and the place of His birth; famous verse about what God expects of man (6:8).	
Nahum	A psalm about the majesty of God; an ode celebrating the fall of Nineveh.	

Habakkuk

A prophet's search to find a reason why God allows the existence of evil and injustice; Nahum's conclusion that trust in God makes one happier than faith in possessions or power.

Zephaniah

A prophecy to Judah of God's anger and judgment upon Jerusalem, followed by a promise of blessings.

Haggai

A message to the restored community in Jerusalem to encourage them to complete the rebuilding of the Temple.

Zechariah

A message to the restored community at Jerusalem to encourage the people to serve God; prophecy of the coming of the Messiah, His rejection, and final triumph.

Malachi

An attempt to renew the religious enthusiasm of disillusioned people in Jerusalem after the return from Babylon; prophecy of the coming of Jesus and John the Baptist.

BOOKS OF THE BIBLE

NEW TESTAMENT (27 Books)

NAME	CONTENT	FAMOUS CHARACTERS
Matthew	Genealogy of Jesus; Jesus' birth and childhood; His baptism; Sermon on the Mount; parables; His instructions to the disciples; Crucifixion and Resurrection.	Mary and Joseph, John the Baptist, the twelve disciples, Caiaphas, Herod, Pilate, Barabbas
Mark	Jesus' ministry, beginning with His baptism; parables; detailed account of the last week; Crucifixion and Resurrection.	John the Baptist, the twelve disciples, Jairus, Bartimaeus, Mary Magdalene, Pilate
Luke	Most orderly account of Jesus' life, beginning with His birth; John the Baptist's birth; parables; Crucifixion and Resurrection.	Mary and Joseph, Gabriel, Elisabeth and Zacharias, John the Baptist, the twelve disciples, Jairus, Lazarus, Mary, Martha, Zacchaeus, Pilate, Cleophas
John	Biographical account of Jesus' life, emphasizing the spiritual importance of Jesus; many miracles and teachings not found in the other Gospels; Crucifixion and Resurrection.	John the Baptist, Lazarus, Mary, Martha, Nicodemus, the twelve disciples

Book	Description	
Acts	Story of the early Christian church; account of Paul's conversion and ministry.	Eleven disciples, Matthias, Ananias, Sapphira, Stephen, Paul, Barnabas, Cornelius, Dorcas, Mark, Silas, Timothy, Eutychus
Romans	Paul's complete explanation to the Romans of the basic truths of Christianity.	
1 Corinthians	Paul's advice on Christian behavior and spiritual gifts; the "love chapter" (13).	
2 Corinthians	Paul's account of his own ministry; advice to the Corinthians about their problems; suggestions for Christian living.	
Galatians	Paul's autobiography defending his apostleship; Paul's teaching that Christ came to free men from the old Jewish laws—now they could be received by God through faith in Christ, not by obeying the laws; the fruits of the Spirit.	
Ephesians	A summary of Paul's teachings about church unity and the Christian "family"; the "armor of God."	
Phillippians	Paul's advice from prison on how to live the Christian life.	

BOOK	CONTENT	FAMOUS CHARACTERS
Colossians	Paul's warnings from prison about letting pagan beliefs creep back into the church; declaration of Christ's supreme power; instructions on Christian morals.	
1 Thessalonians	Paul's encouragement to those suffering persecution; standards for behavior of the church.	
2 Thessalonians	Paul's instructions on Christ's second coming and warnings about idleness before He arrives.	
1 Timothy	Paul's advice about the problems of church life such as behavior in public worship, church government and its leaders, and relationships between believers.	
2 Timothy	Paul's expression of personal feelings about his own life; warnings about distressing times to come and how to make it through them.	
Titus	Paul's message about stewardship; counsel on qualifications and duties of ministers; advice on Christian conduct.	

Philemon	Paul's request that a runaway slave be forgiven and taken back as a Christian brother.	Onesimus
Hebrews	Argument for Christianity over Judaism; practical instructions for believers; the "faith" chapter (11).	
James	James' short, proverbial sayings; advice about Christian behavior; encouragement to show faith through works.	
1 Peter	Peter's message of hope to suffering Christians; advice about life at home and in the world.	
2 Peter	Peter's steps for growing strong spiritually; warnings against false teachers.	
1 John	John's instructions for living pure lives based on belief in Christ and brotherly love.	
2 John	John's warnings against teachers promoting divisions in the church.	
3 John	John's request to Gaius, a loyal friend, to welcome missionaries.	
Jude	Message warning of heretics in the church; beautiful doxology in closing.	
Revelation	A prophetic look at things to come and at God's final victory over all evil forces of the world.	

THE BOOKS OF THE BIBLE

OLD TESTAMENT (39 Books)

Law:
Genesis
Exodus
Leviticus
Numbers
Deuteronomy

History:
Joshua
Judges
Ruth
1 Samuel
2 Samuel
1 Kings
2 Kings
1 Chronicles
2 Chronicles
Ezra
Nehemiah
Esther

Poetry and Prose:
Job
Psalms
Proverbs
Ecclesiastes
Song of Solomon

Prophecy:
Isaiah
Jeremiah
Lamentations
Ezekiel
Daniel
Hosea
Joel
Amos
Obadiah
Jonah
Micah
Nahum
Habakkuk
Zephaniah
Haggai
Zechariah
Malachi

NEW TESTAMENT (27 Books)

Gospels (Life of Jesus):
Matthew
Mark
Luke
John

Beginning of the Christian Church
Acts

Epistles (Letters):
Romans
1 Corinthians
2 Corinthians
Galatians
Ephesians
Philippians
Colossians
1 Thessalonians
2 Thessalonians
1 Timothy
2 Timothy
Titus
Philemon
Hebrews
James
1 Peter
2 Peter
1 John
2 John
3 John
Jude

Prophecy:
The Revelation

FEASTS AND FESTIVALS

Jewish Holidays

Seven feasts are commanded by God in Leviticus 23. They are still observed by Jewish families. To know about Jewish holidays can only bring a greater understanding of the Jewish roots of our Christian faith.

Passover
- celebrates the enslaved Israelites' oldest child being "passed over" while those of their Egyptian masters were slain
- held on the night before the Feast of Unleavened Bread
- the Last Supper was a Passover meal

Feast of Unleavened Bread
- lasts a week, beginning the morning after Passover
- observed to remember the Israelites' rapid exit from Egypt. They left so fast there was not time to add leaven to the bread to make it rise.
- a time when only unleavened bread (matzo) is eaten

Feast of First Fruits
- celebrated on the second day of the Feast of Unleavened Bread
- an agricultural holiday of thanksgiving for the barley harvest
- celebrated as a sign of a productive growing season

Feast of Weeks or Pentecost (Shavuot)
- comes fifty days after the Passover
- an agricultural feast of thanksgiving for the wheat harvest
- is the day the Holy Spirit came on the disciples and, therefore, marks the birth of the Christian church

85

Feast of Trumpets (Rosh Hashanah)

- occurs in the autumn
- Jewish New Year's Day
- got its name because God called for the blowing of trumpets on this day to call the Israelites together for a serious meeting
- the first day of ten days of repentance

Day of Atonement (Yom Kippur)

- occurs on the tenth day of the Feast of Trumpets
- a day of fasting and praying for forgiveness and reunion with God

Feast of Booths (Succoth)

- held at the close of the agricultural season in Bible times
- brought together in Jerusalem all Jews who were able
- got its name from people living seven days in temporary "booths" made of branches in remembrance of the Israelites' wanderings in the wilderness

Other Bible-Time celebrations:

Sabbatical Year

- observed every seventh year
- the ground would rest this year, for God promised the sixth year would provide enough food for two years.

Jubilee Year

- came at the end of seven sabbatical years (or every 50th year)
- slaves were freed and property that had been sold because of poverty was returned

Feast of Lights or Feast of Dedication (Hanukkah)

- celebrates a victory over the Syrians in 165 B.C. after which the Temple in Jerusalem was rededicated to God
- celebrates the lighting of the holy lamps in the Temple with a very small cruse of oil which miraculously lasted eight days
- on each day one candle of the menorah (candelabra) is lighted
- now a time of gift exchange and contributions to the poor, and usually falls in the month of December

SPECIAL PARTIES

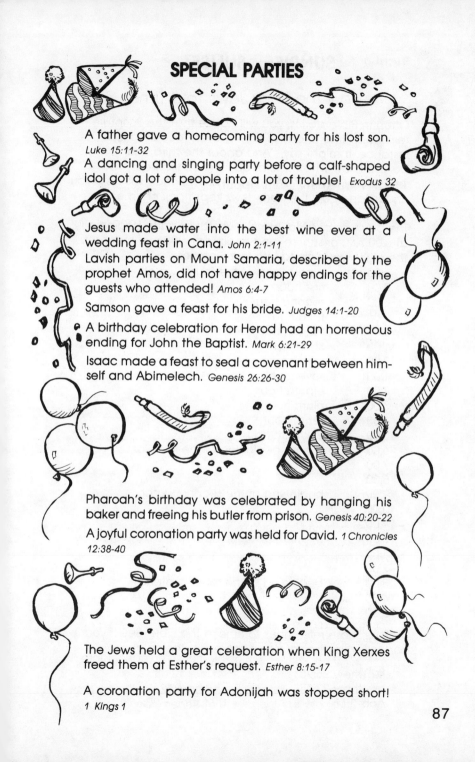

A father gave a homecoming party for his lost son.
Luke 15:11-32

A dancing and singing party before a calf-shaped idol got a lot of people into a lot of trouble! *Exodus 32*

Jesus made water into the best wine ever at a wedding feast in Cana. *John 2:1-11*

Lavish parties on Mount Samaria, described by the prophet Amos, did not have happy endings for the guests who attended! *Amos 6:4-7*

Samson gave a feast for his bride. *Judges 14:1-20*

A birthday celebration for Herod had an horrendous ending for John the Baptist. *Mark 6:21-29*

Isaac made a feast to seal a covenant between himself and Abimelech. *Genesis 26:26-30*

Pharoah's birthday was celebrated by hanging his baker and freeing his butler from prison. *Genesis 40:20-22*

A joyful coronation party was held for David. *1 Chronicles 12:38-40*

The Jews held a great celebration when King Xerxes freed them at Esther's request. *Esther 8:15-17*

A coronation party for Adonijah was stopped short!
1 Kings 1

SUNRISE...SUNSET

How the Early Jews Told Time

Often in Bible stories, you will notice that the Scripture tells what time of day a story or event occurred. For instance, it might say, "And about the third hour..." Do you know what time of day is the third hour? The Jewish day was not quite like ours. This chart will help you understand how the early Jews kept track of time.

The day was divided into twelve equal parts, beginning at 6:00 A.M., or sunrise, and ending at 6:00 P.M., or sunset. The night was divided into four watches.

6:00 A.M.	sunrise, end of the fourth watch
7:00	first hour
8:00	second hour
9:00	third hour
10:00	fourth hour
11:00	fifth hour
12:00 P.M.	sixth hour - noon
1:00	seventh hour
2:00	eighth hour
3:00	ninth hour
4:00	tenth hour
5:00	eleventh hour
6:00	sunset, beginning of the first watch
7:00	
8:00	
9:00	beginning of the second watch
10:00	
11:00	
12:00 A.M.	midnight, beginning of the third watch
1:00	
2:00	
3:00	beginning of the fourth watch
4:00	
5:00	

Look for these references to time in the Bible. See if you can tell what time of day each event took place.

Matthew 26:75	Luke 12:38
Matthew 27:45	John 4:52
Acts 2:15	Matthew 20:6

JOBS, TRADES, CRAFTS & PROFESSIONS

What Folks Did For Work

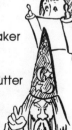

archer	hairdresser	queen
armorbearer	harpist	rabbi
astrologer	herald	reaper
athlete	horseman	recorder
baker	hunter	robber
banker	innkeeper	Sadducee
beggar	interpreter	sailor
bishop	jailor	scribe
blacksmith	judge	sculptor
bodyguard	king	servant
bricklayer	lawyer	shepherd
builder	leathermaker	silversmith
butcher	magician	singer
carpenter	maidservant	snake charmer
census taker	mason	soldier
centurion	merchant	sorcerer
chariot driver	messenger	sower
cook	midwife	spy
courier	minister	standard bearer
cupbearer	minstrel	stonecutter
dancer	money changer	tanner
disciple	mother	tax collector
doctor	mourner	teacher
drummer	musician	tent maker
eunuch	Pharisee	treasurer
evangelist	policeman	watchman
farmer	porter	weaver
fisherman	potter	wife
foreman	priest	winemaker
fortune-teller	prime minister	witch
gardener	prince	wizard
gatekeeper	princess	woodcutter
governor	prophet	
grave digger	prophetess	

THEY SAID .... WE SAY

Shekels, talents, mites, pounds	Dimes, nickels, quarters, dollars
Winebibber	Drunkard
Swine	Pigs
Tares	Weeds
Sepulcher	Tomb, Grave
Latchet	Shoelace
Kine	Cows
Mess	Dish (of food)
Crisping Pins	Curling Irons
Looking Glass	Mirror
Espoused	Engaged
Fetters	Chains
Husbandman	Farmer
Charger	Platter
Besom	Broom
Waxed	Grew
Lucre	Money
Potsherd	Memo Pads
Chaff	Straw
Money Changers	Bankers
Ass	Donkey
Leviathan	Sea Monster
Scribe	Secretary
Epistle	Letter
Mantle	Cape
Thee, Thou	You
Pottage	Soup
Sowing	Planting
Patriarch	Father
Blessed	Happy
Covenant	Promise
Hallowed	Honored
Manifest	Show
Firstborn	Oldest

SO WHAT'S A CUBIT???

A List of Approximate Measures

LENGTH

Cubit—distance from elbow to fingertip (17.5 inches)
Finger—width of a finger (3/4 inch); 1/4 handbreadth
Handbreadth or Palm—width of hand at the base of the fingers (3 inches)
Span—from tip of little finger to tip of thumb with hand stretched out (9 inches)
Pace—one giant step (1 yard)
Reed—6 cubits (3 yards)
Mile—1,615 yards or about 9/10 of the modern mile
Day's Journey—15 to 20 miles
Sabbath Day's Journey—1-1/2 miles

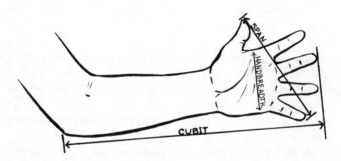

AREA

Yoke—area of ground a pair of oxen could plow in a day

LIQUID MEASURE

Log—2/3 pint
Kab—1-1/4 quarts or 5 cups
Hin—1 gallon
Bath—5 gallons and 1 pint
Homer—10 baths or 1 donkey load

DRY MEASURE

Log—1 cup
Kab—1 quart
Omer—2 quarts
Seah—6-1/2 quarts
Ephah—3-1/2 pecks
Homer—8 bushels or 1 donkey load

IMPORTANT BIBLE CITIES

Antioch—Paul and Barnabas preached here; disciples were first called Christians here.

Athens—Capital city of Greece.

Babylon—Capital city of the Babylonian Empire.

Bethany—Home of Lazarus, Martha, Mary, and Simon the leper.

Bethlehem—Place of Jesus' birth; hometown of David, Ruth, Boaz, Obed.

Caesarea—Home of Cornelius and Philip, the evangelist; place where Paul was tried before Festus and Agrippa.

Caesarea Philippi—The city where Jesus asked Peter, "Who do men say that I am?"

Cana—Where Jesus performed his first miracle—water to wine—about four miles from Nazareth.

Capernaum—Jesus' "second hometown"; the city where he healed the centurion's servant, Peter's mother-in-law, the man lowered through the rooftop by his friends, and others. He found the apostle Matthew here. When people would not repent, Jesus predicted the ruin of the city.

Damascus—Capital city of Syria; Saul was converted on his way to this place.

Jericho—Important city in the Jordan valley; the place where Joshua's company tumbled its walls with marching and trumpets; where Jesus healed Bartimaeus, Zacchaeus was saved, and Achan looted.

Jerusalem—The Holy City; capital city of Judah; place of the Crucifixion.

Nazareth—Place of Jesus' boyhood home.

Nineveh—Capital city of Assyria; God sent Jonah here to evangelize.

Rome—Capital of the Roman Empire.

Sodom & Gomorrah—Twin cities destroyed by fire from heaven because of their wickedness; only Lot's family survived.

Tarsus—Birthplace of Paul.

MOUNTAINS TO REMEMBER

Mount Ararat—The place where Noah's ark came to rest after the flood.

Mount Carmel—Scene of Elijah's contest with the prophets of Baal.

Mount of Jesus' Sermon (*Matthew 5*)—A mountain near Galilee where Jesus preached the Sermon on the Mount (the Beatitudes). The exact location is not known.

Mount Moriah—The place where Abraham offered Isaac as a sacrifice; later, the site of Solomon's temple.

Mount of Olives—Very near to Jerusalem on the east; the Garden of Gethsemane lies on its slopes; place from which Jesus ascended into heaven (*Acts 1:12*).

Mount Sinai—The place where the Ten Commandments were given to Moses and the people worshipped the golden calf.

Mount of Transfiguration (perhaps Mount Hermon)—The place where Jesus talked with Moses and Elijah whose glorified bodies reappeared from the dead (*Matthew 17:1-9*).

Mount Zion—One of the hills of Jerusalem to which David brought the ark of the covenant.

BODIES OF WATER

Cherith Brook—A brook by Jordan from which Elijah drank; where he was fed by ravens during the famine.

Dead Sea (Sea of Salt)—Lowest surface on the globe; saltier than the oceans; fed by the river Jordan.

Euphrates River—Called the Great River; flowed out of the Garden of Eden; Babylon built on its banks.

Jordan River—Place of Jesus' Baptism; where Naaman dipped seven times to get rid of leprosy; once divided for the Israelites to cross.

Mediterranean Sea (the Great Sea)—The sea which lies between Europe and Africa.

Red Sea—The sea which rolled back to allow the Israelites to flee from the Egyptians.

Sea of Galilee—Where Jesus called his disciples; where he preached from a boat; where he slept through a storm that frightened his disciples; where Peter walked to meet him on the water.

ALL ABOUT ANGELS

Some Things the Bible Tells About Them

1. They were created by God. *Genesis 2:1*

2. There are several orders or classes. *Isaiah 6:2* (Some are "higher" or more important than others.)

3. They are immortal. (They don't die.) *Luke 20:36*

4. They worship God. *Philippians 2:9-11*

5. They are obedient. *Matthew 6:10*

6. They do not marry. *Matthew 22:30*

7. There are many thousands of them. *Deuteronomy 33:2*

8. Only three are actually named in the Bible—Gabriel, Michael, Lucifer.

9. Some are fallen. (They left God and decided to be bad angels. Lucifer is the only one whose name we know.)

10. They have personalities and are not just forces. *Luke 1:26*

11. They can appear in visible form. *Luke 1:12*

12. They help people. *Hebrews 1:14*

REAL PEOPLE WHO SAW
REAL ANGELS

Lot—Genesis 19:1-22
Hagar—Genesis 21:17
Abraham—Genesis 22:11, 12
Jacob—Genesis 28:10-19 (He wrestled with one!)
Moses—Exodus 3:2
Balaam—Numbers 22:21-35 (His donkey saw it first!)
Joshua—Joshua 5:14
Gideon—Judges 6:11-22
Manoah and his wife—Judges 13 (announcement of Samson's birth)
David—2 Samuel 24:17
Elijah—1 Kings 19:5
Shadrach, Meshach, Abednego and Nebuchadnezzar—Daniel 3:25-28
Daniel—Daniel 6:21, 22
Zechariah—Zechariah 1-6
Joseph—Matthew 1:20, 21 (announcement of Jesus' birth)
—Matthew 2:13 (warning to escape to Egypt with baby Jesus)
Mary—Luke 1:26-38 (announcement of Jesus' birth)
Zacharias—Luke 1:5-25 (announcement of John the Baptist's birth)
Shepherds—Luke 2:8-14 (announcement of Jesus' birth)
Jesus—Matthew 4:11 (after the temptation)
Women at Jesus' tomb—Matthew 28:2-6
Apostles at the Ascension—Acts 1: 10, 11
Peter and John in prison—Acts 5:19
Philip at Samaria—Acts 8:26
Cornelius—Acts 10:1-8
Peter, in prison—Acts 12:7-10
Paul, on the road to Damascus—Acts 27:23
John, in Patmos—Revelation 1:1, 5:2-7

So who says angels aren't real????????

95

MENE MENE TEKE

UNIQUE WRITING MATERIALS

In modern days, most writing is done on paper. Paper was not always available in Bible times, but even when it was, other strange materials were often written upon. Look up each reference below to get the full story.

    a gold plate—Exodus 39:30
    sticks—Ezekiel 37:16-20
    a wall—Daniel 5:1-30
    a rod—Numbers 17:3
    plastered stones—Deuteronomy 27:2
    the thigh of "faithful and true"—Revelation 19:12, 16
    houseposts—Deuteronomy 6:9
    doorposts—Exodus 12:21-23
    gates—Deuteronomy 11:20
    a woman's forehead—Revelation 17:5
    broken pieces of pottery—Job 2:8
    earth—Jeremiah 17:13

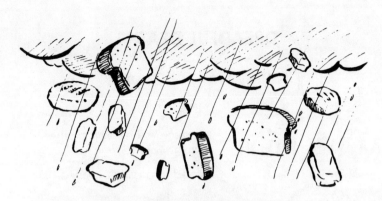

EXTRAORDINARY ACTS
OF NATURE

It rains nonstop for forty days and nights *Genesis 7, 8*
A storm stops when a man is thrown overboard. *Jonah 1:12-15*
Fire from heaven consumes water and meat. *1 Kings 18:38, 39*
Twin cities are destroyed, and a woman turns to salt.
     Genesis 19
Bread rains from heaven. *Exodus 16:4-31*
Quail are blown in from the sea. *Exodus 16:13*
A sea divides to make a dry path. *Exodus 14:21, 22*
The sun and moon stand still. *Joshua 10:12-14*
Dew appears all around a dry fleece. *Judges 6:37-40*
The Jordan River divides. *Joshua 3:14-17*
Hail falls on kings. *Joshua 10:11*
A huge vine grows to shade Jonah, then withers. *Jonah 4:5-10*
The sky is dark at noon and the earth shakes at the
     Crucifixion. *Matthew 27:45-51*
Thunder and lightning accompany the giving of the law.
     Exodus 19:16-20
A sundial moves backward ten degrees. *Isaiah 38*

DREADFUL DEATHS

Not By Natural Causes

ABEL — Murdered by his own brother, Cain. *Genesis 4:2*

LOT'S WIFE — Turned to a pillar of salt. *Genesis 19:26*

PHAROAH'S CHIEF BAKER — Hanged as Joseph predicted. *Genesis 40:22*

NADAB, ABIHU — Aaron's sons who burned when fire blazed from the altar. *Leviticus 10:12*

SABBATH BREAKER — Stoned for picking up sticks on the Sabbath day. *Numbers 15:32-36*

ACHAN — Stoned for stealing from the conquered people of Jericho. *Joshua 7:20-25*

KING EGLON — Stabbed with a double-edged knife, more than 16 inches long. *Judges 3:21, 22*

SISERA — Had a long spike driven through his brain. *Judges 5:26*

ABIMELECH — Fatally wounded when a woman dropped a rock on his head but, not wanting anyone to say a woman did him in, he ordered one of his soldiers to run him through with his sword. *Judges 9:51-54*

1000 PHILISTINES — Killed by Samson with the jawbone of a donkey. *Judges 15:15*

SAMSON — Hit by a crumbling building he himself caused to fall. *Judges 16:29, 30*

SAUL   Leaped on his own sword after
        being fatally wounded by
        Philistine archers. *1 Samuel 31:3,*

UZZAH   Died when he touched the ark
        of the covenant to steady it.
        2 Samuel 6:6, 7

ABSALOM   Yanked off his mule when his
                    hair caught a tree branch, and
                    then had three darts thrust
                    through his heart as he dangled
                    there. *2 Samuel 18:9-15*

AMASA   Run through by a sword, thinking
                    he was to receive only a kiss from
                    his assassin. *2 Samuel 20:9, 10*

SEVEN SONS OF SAUL Hanged as a sacrifice by the
                    Gibeonites as revenge against
                    Saul. *2 Samuel 21:6-8*

NABOTH   Stoned to death because Ahab
                    wanted his vineyard. *1 Kings 21:13*

ZIMRI   King for seven days, he set fire
                    to his palace and burned
                    himself to death. *1 Kings 16:18*

AHAB   Hit by an arrow in battle; the
                    dogs licked up his blood as
                    Elijah had said they would.
                    1 Kings 22:34-38

JEZEBEL   Thrown from a window, trampled
                    by horses, and eaten by dogs.
                    2 Kings 9:30-37

99

URIAH	Sent to the front lines of battle by David. *2 Samuel 11:14-17*
AHAZIAH OF ISRAEL	Fatally wounded when he fell through a lattice in his upper room. *2 Kings 1:1-16*
HAMAN	Hung on the gallows he built for Mordecai. *Esther 9:25*
JOHN THE BAPTIST	His head was served on a silver platter as a reward for Salome after she danced for the king. *Mark 6:17-28*
JESUS	Allowed Himself to be crucified unjustly to pay for the sins of the world. *Matthew 27:35*
JUDAS ISCARIOT	Hanged himself after giving the thirty pieces of silver back to the priests. *Matthew 27:3-5*
ANANIAS AND SAPPHIRA	Dropped dead after lying to the Holy Spirit. *Acts 5:1-10*
STEPHEN	Stoned for being a Christian. *Acts 7:59*

EUTYCHUS	Fell out of a window while he slept through Paul's long-winded sermon; he was revived by Paul. *Acts 20:9-19*
HEROD, AGRIPPA I	Died of worms. *Acts 12:21-23*
GOLIATH	Hit by a stone from a sling. *1 Samuel 17*

AMAZING FACTS

(Please be amazed!!!! Here's how... Open your eyes and mouth wide with surprise and gasp, "I didn't know that!!!")

- Some of Goliath's relatives had 12 fingers and toes. *2 Samuel 21:20*

- In the Old Testament, Nazareth was considered unimportant and was never mentioned.

- A young girl named Rhoda ran excitedly to announce Peter's arrival and forgot to open the door for him. *Acts 12*

- Hebrew is written right to left.

- Jews did not celebrate their birthdays.

- Moses sweetened water too bitter to drink by throwing a tree in it. *Exodus 15:22-25*

- God ate pancakes with Abraham and Sarah. *Genesis 18:2-5*

- Not one fish is named in the Bible.

- An inner gate to a city is called a needle's eye (probably because it was so small, it was hard for a camel to go through).

- Bodies of criminals were not usually buried, but were left for the dogs and vultures.

- In the time of the Old Testament, the oldest son received twice as much inheritance as a younger son.

- Jews did not eat with silverware, but used a piece of bread and their fingers to pick up their food.

- The bodies of newborn babies were rubbed with salt. (What a welcoming!)

- Only wealthy people had chairs in their homes. Others sat on their floor.

- Joshua killed 31 kings. *Joshua 12:24*

- The sun and the moon stood still to wait for Joshua to win a battle. *Joshua 10:1-27*

- Judas' 30 pieces of silver were used to buy a cemetery because it was "blood money."

- The Olympic games started in Old Testament times—776 B.C.

- Notes and letters were sometimes written on old, broken pieces of pottery.

- Solomon wrote 3,000 proverbs and 1,005 songs. *1 Kings 4:32*
- Moses spent about one-third of his life as a shepherd.
- A manger was usually a stone box.
- Balaam had a talking donkey. *Numbers 22:28-31*
- Solomon had 40,000 stalls of horses. *1 Kings 4:26*
- Most of the gospel of John does not appear in the other three Gospels.
- God is not mentioned in the book of Esther.
- King Hanun thought David's servants were spying on him so he cut the back ends out of their clothes and sent them home exposed (and probably embarrassed). *1 Chronicles 19:1-5*
- In Palestine, families had two meals a day—one in late morning and the main meal in the evening.
- The Israelites wandered in the wilderness for 40 years, but their clothes and shoes never wore out. *Deuteronomy 29:5*

MARK-A-MAP

- Draw a line from the place of Jesus' boyhood home to the place of his very first miracle.
- Place a star near the city of Jesus' birth.
- Draw a jagged line around the city whose walls tumbled at the obedience of Joshua's army.
- Put an X on the body of water where Naaman got rid of his leprosy.
- Place a cross near the city where Jesus was crucified.
- Draw a tiny house by the home of Mary, Martha, and Lazarus.
- Circle the city where Paul was tried by Festus and Agrippa.
- Color in the body of water where Peter walked on the water and Jesus stilled the storm.
- Make a heart shape around the city that was Jesus' "second hometown"—where he found Matthew and healed many people. *(Answers on Page 136)*

ISRAEL DURING THE TIME OF CHRIST'S MINISTRY

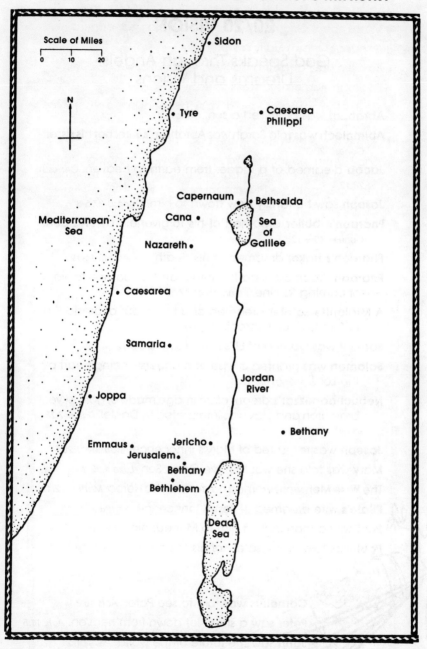

20/20 VISION

God Speaks Through Angels, Dreams and Visions

Abraham was promised a son. *Genesis 17:16*

Abimelech was told Sarah was Abraham's wife, not his sister. *Genesis 20:3*

Jacob dreamed of a ladder from earth to heaven. *Genesis 28:12*

Joseph saw his family bow down to him. *Genesis 37:5-8*

Pharaoh's butler dreamed of his forgiveness by Pharaoh. *Genesis 40:9-13*

Pharaoh's baker dreamed of his death. *Genesis 40:16-19*

Pharaoh dreamed of cattle (interpreted by Joseph to warn of coming famine.) *Genesis 41:17-32*

A Midianite soldier dreamed of a huge loaf of bread just before Gideon's attack. *Judges 7:13*

Samuel was warned of Eli's sons. *1 Samuel 3:5-12*

Solomon was granted a wise and understanding heart by the Lord. *1 Kings 3:5-12*

Nebuchadnezzar's dream of an image made of gold, silver, brass, iron and clay was interpreted by Daniel. *Daniel 2:28-45*

Joseph was reassured of Mary's innocence. *Matthew 1:20*

Mary was told she would have God's Son. *Luke 1:30-35*

The Wise Men were warned not to return to Herod. *Matthew 2:12*

Pilate's wife dreamed of Jesus' innocence. *Matthew 27:19*

Paul saw a man calling him to Macedonia. *Acts 16:9*

Paul was told of the safety of his shipmates. *Acts 27:24*

Cornelius was told to see Peter. *Acts 10:3*

Peter saw a sheet let down from heaven. *Acts 11:5*

John saw the future of the world. *Revelation*

GOOD REASONS TO GO TO CHURCH

- God says so! *Hebrews 10:25*
- It's a great place to find Christian friends.
- It is good to worship God as a group of believers rather than alone all the time.
- It's a way to show your world that spiritual things are important to you.
- You need to be associated with other Christians.
- You need to love and encourage other brothers and sisters in Christ.
- You need to be a part of a group that can have some good influence in our world.
- The church offers good opportunities for Christian service to needy people.
- Church is a good place to develop skills and talents that can be used in Christian service.
- It's a good place to find some quiet time to say "I love you!" to God.

_____

_____

_____

_____

Use these lines to add some reasons of your own.

SUPERLATIVES

FIRST child to be born - Cain

OLDEST man - Methuselah

Book with the FEWEST number of verses - 2 John

One of the STRONGEST men in the Bible - Samson

One of the LARGEST men in the Bible (over 9 feet tall) - Goliath

One of the SHORTEST men in the Bible - Zacchaeus

Wrote the MOST books in the Bible (13 or 14) - Paul

Israel's FIRST king - Saul

Judah's YOUNGEST king - Joash (7 years old)

Jesus' FIRST miracle - Water to wine *John 2:1-12*

FIRST gentile to become a Christian - Cornelius

Bible's two BEST KNOWN songwriters - David and Solomon

FIRST book in the Bible - Genesis

FIRST murderer - Cain

LAST book in the Bible - Revelation

Perhaps Israel's MEANEST king - Manasseh

Perhaps Israel's KINDEST king - Solomon

World's BEST-SELLING book - Bible

Perhaps the WICKEDEST grandmother ever - Athaliah

LOWEST place on the earth - Dead Sea (3,000 feet below sea level)

LONGEST name in the Bible - Ma-her-shal-al-hash-baz *Isaiah 8:1*

GROSSEST gift in the Bible - John the Baptist's head on a platter (given to Salome by Herod Antipas)

SHORTEST verse in the Bible - John 11:35 (two words)

LONGEST verse in the Bible - Esther 8:9 (90 words in the King James Version)

FIRST mother - Eve

LAST book in the Old Testament - Malachi

FIRST book in the New Testament - Matthew

MOST COMMON name in the Bible - Zechariah (used more than 30 times)

MOST COMMON word in the English versions of the Bible - and Jesus' LAST words on the cross - "It is finished."

FASTEST trip to heaven - Elijah, taken into heaven "by a whirlwind" *2 Kings 2:1, 11*

FIRST command recorded in the Bible - "Be fruitful and multiply." *Genesis 1:27*

106

Bible's MOST UNUSUAL living accommodations - The belly of
    a fish (Jonah)

Winner of the FIRST beauty contest - Queen Esther *Esther 2*
FIRST Christian martyr - Stephen *Acts 6:7 - 8:3*
HIGHEST or MOST IMPORTANT angels named in the Bible -
    Gabriel, Michael
MIDDLE verse in the Bible - Psalm 118:8
FIRST and MOST UNUSUAL Bible birthday party - Pharoah of
    Egypt during Joseph's time gave a party for his servants.
    He freed his head butler from jail and hanged his chief
    baker. *Genesis 40:20-22*
MOST DISASTROUS suicide-murder - Samson (He killed
    himself about 6,000 Philistines when he destroyed the
    Philistine temple.)
MOST HIDEOUS "decoration" mentioned in the Bible - King
    Saul's head hung in the temple of Dagon by the
    Philistines *1 Chronicles 10:10*
FIRST parable in the Bible - Told by Gideon's youngest son,
    Jotham *Judges 9*
FIRST missionary - Paul
SHORTEST book in the Old Testament - Obadiah
Probably the OLDEST city in the world - Jericho
Definitely, the world's BIGGEST liar ever - Satan

ANIMAL HEADLINES

Some Of The World's
Best Animal Stories

LISTEN TO THE LETTERS

Can you decipher these names and write them correctly in the space beside each one? The list below will help you with spelling. (It is not in the proper order!)

ADD 'EM   _____

FILL UP   _____

HEY, MAN!   _____

MO SAYS   _____

BAIL   _____

TOE MASS   _____

SAM YULE   _____

RAY CHILL   _____

PILE LOT   _____

NEIGH, BULL   _____

NAME ANN   _____

MARRY HIM   _____

A CAN   _____

MATH YOU   _____

JAW SHOE AH   _____

A BULL   _____

JAY CUB   _____

A BEAGLE   _____

SACK KEY US   _____

EYE SACK   _____

AIR RAN   _____

GIDDY ANN   _____

HAIR ODD   _____

BAR KNEE BUS   _____

DOOR CASE   _____

DAN, YELL!   _____

Zacchaeus, Thomas, Isaac, Samuel, Herod, Rachel, Gideon, Pilate, Dorcas, Nabal, Daniel, Barnabas, Naaman, Miriam, Adam, Matthew, Philip, Baal, Joshua, Achan, Haman, Abel, Moses, Aaron, Jacob, Abigail, Sarah

109

PLAGUES

One Way God Disciplines People Who Ignore Him

God often used plagues—horrible diseases or great disasters—to convince people that He meant what He said. The first plague mentioned in the Bible was one He caused to happen to the Egyptian Pharaoh because he took Abraham's wife, Sarah, to be his wife. God used the plague to protect Sarah. The king sent Abraham and Sarah away quickly.

The ten Egyptian plagues were God's way of telling Pharaoh how serious He was about letting Moses and the Israelites go from Egypt. This list tells all the things God did to get Pharaoh's attention. Old Pharaoh must have been a real slow learner!!

1. River waters turn to **blood**.
2. **Frogs** are everywhere!
3. **Lice** invade everything.
4. Swarms of biting **flies** arrive.
5. A **virus** kills all the cattle.
6. All the men and animals get **boils**.
7. There are great **hailstorms**.
8. **Locusts** cover the ground, trees and houses.
9. There is total **darkness**.
10. The **firstborn** of every family **dies**.

You can read this story in Exodus 7:14–12:50.

Sometimes God punished His own people with plagues when they disobeyed Him.

- A plague was sent upon the Israelites for worshipping a golden calf idol

- A plague was punishment for grumping about the food God gave them in the wilderness.

- Spies died of a plague for bringing back bad reports and making the people feel discouraged and unhappy.

- Thousands of people died because they were immortal and worshipped idols.

- The Philistines suffered with a plague of tumors when they stole the ark of the covenant.

- David chose a plague as punishment for his sin. Seventy thousand of David's soldiers died before he built an altar and asked God to stop the plague.

WHO SAID...??

1. "Speak, Lord, for thy servant heareth." *1 Samuel 3:10*
2. "Be sure your sin will find you out." *Numbers 32:23*
3. "Ye shall not surely die." *Genesis 3:4*
4. "Freely ye have received, freely give." *Matthew 10:8*
5. "I am the voice of one crying in the wilderness, Make straight the way of the Lord." *John 1:23*
6. "Lord, teach us to pray." *Luke 11:1*
7. "If I perish, I perish." *Esther 4:16*
8. "I know that my redeemer liveth." *Job 19:25*
9. "For God so loved the world, that he gave his only be-gotten Son, that whosoever believeth in him should not perish, but have everlasting life." *John 3:16*
10. "As for me and my house, we will serve the Lord." *Joshua 24:15*
11. "Entreat me not to leave thee." *Ruth 1:16*
12. "Cast thy burden upon the Lord, and he shall sustain thee." *Psalm 55:22*
13. "A merry heart doeth good like a medicine." *Proverbs 17:22*
14. "For I am not ashamed of the gospel of Christ." *Romans 1:16*
15. "Father, forgive them; for they know not what they do." *Luke 23:34*
16. "Lord, lay not this sin to their charge." *Acts 7:59, 60*
17. "The tongue can no man tame." *James 3:8*
18. "Silver and gold have I none; but such as I have, give I thee." *Acts 3:6*
19. "Though your sins be as scarlet, they shall be as white as snow." *Isaiah 1:18*
20. "He that is not with me is against me." *Matthew 12:30*

ANSWERS:

1. Samuel 2. Moses 3. Serpent 4. Jesus 5. John the Baptist 6. Disciples 7. Esther 8. Job 9. Jesus 10. Joshua 11. Ruth 12. David 13. probably Solomon 14. Paul 15. Jesus 16. Stephen 17. James 18. Peter 19. Isaiah 20. Jesus

SIGNS AND WONDERS

All through the Bible, God's power is shown through special signs and wonders. Here are a few of them. See if you can add some more to the list!

A rainbow—*Genesis 9:12-14*
A brass serpent—*Numbers 21:6-9*
A withered hand—*1 Kings 13*
A shadow on a sundial—*Isaiah 38*
A burning bush—*Exodus 3:2*
A rod that changes to a serpent—*Exodus 7:10*
A rod that buds—*Numbers 17:8*
A donkey who speaks—*Numbers 22:28*
An ax head that floats—*2 Kings 6:5*
A piece of meat burned by fire from heaven—*1 Kings 18:38*
The sun and moon stopped still—*Joshua 10:12*
A chariot of fire that takes a man to heaven—*2 Kings 2:9-15*
A pillar of cloud and a pillar of fire—*Exodus 13:21, 22*
A babe wrapped in swaddling clothes—*Luke 2:12*
A fleece, wet, then dry—*Judges 6:37-40*
A serpent that swallows other serpents—*Exodus 7:5-12*
Two special cows who return the ark of the covenant—
  1 Samuel 6:1-21

_____

_____

_____

_____

_____

A B C STORIES

About Bible Characters

A	Amazement—Balaam	Numbers 22:1-38
B	Betrayal—Delilah	Judges 16:4-31
C	Courage—Gideon	Judges 7:7-23
D	Devotion—Ruth	Ruth 1:1-18
E	Earthquake—Paul	Acts 16:11-40
F	Fire—Shadrach, Meshach, Abednego	Daniel 3
G	Greed—Achan	Joshua 7
H	Heroism—Paul	2 Corinthians 11:23-28
I	Insomnia—Samuel	1 Samuel 3
J	Joy—Jairus	Mark 5:22-43
K	Kindness—Good Samaritan	Luke 10:25-37
L	Love—Jacob	Genesis 29:1-20
M	Meanness—Athaliah	2 Kings 11:1
N	Nourishment—Elijah	1 Kings 17:8-16
O	Obedience—Abraham	Genesis 22:1-18
P	Patience—Job	Job 1;2;42
Q	Quest—Nicodemus	John 3:1-21
R	Rebellion—Absalom	2 Samuel 18
S	Selfishness—Nabal	1 Samuel 25:1-28
T	Trust—Joshua	Joshua 6
U	Unfaithfulness—Bath-sheba	2 Samuel 11:2-27
V	Vanity—Agrippa	Acts 12:1-23
W	Wisdom—Solomon	1 Kings 3:16-23
X	Exit—Moses	Exodus
Y	Youth—Israelite Girl	2 Kings 5
Z	Zest—Zacchaeus	Luke 19:1-10

When you have used the references to find and read the stories listed on this page, you can make a game by covering the names of the Bible characters and trying to remember them. OR you might make up your own ABC word game using new key words and different characters.

TONGUE TRILLS

Some of the Bible's Funnest & Funniest Names to Say

Mephibosheth (me FIB oh sheth)—lame son of Jonathan
Jehoshaphat (jih HAHSH uh fat)—a king of Judah
Michmash (MIK mash)—a city
Methuselah (mih THYOO zuh luh)—the oldest man ever

Mizpah (MIZ pah)—a city   Say these two, one right after
Pisgah (PIZ guh)—a mountain   the other. It's fun!

Og (AHG)—a giant king
Abimelech (uh BIM eh lek)—son of Gideon
Nebuchadnezzar (neb yoo kad NEZZ ur)—a king of Babylon
Jochebed (JOK uh bed)—mother of Miriam, Aaron, and Moses
Habakkuk (huh BAK uhk)—a prophet
Ecclesiastes (eh KLEE zih ass teez)—a book of the Old Testament
Deuteronomy (dyoo tuh RAHN uh mih)—fifth book of the Old Testament
Abednego (uh BED nih go)—a Hebrew friend of Daniel
Melchizedek (mel KIZ uh dek)—a high priest of Israel
Zerubbabel (zuh RUHB uh buhl)—a leader of the Jews

FIFTEEN SHORT, FUNNY NAMES

Ur	Ziph	Ono
Non	Put	No
Nob	Ozni	Nod
Shoco	Nebo	Ziza
Zoba	Zin	Ziz

FISH TALES
YOU CAN BELIEVE!

Jonah spent three days and three nights praying inside the belly of a large fish. He begged God's forgiveness for trying to run away from Him. Finally, God made the fish spit Jonah onto the land so he could go on to Nineveh to help the wicked people there change their ways.

—Book of Jonah

Once Jesus was healing sick people among a crowd of five thousand men, plus women and children. When dinnertime came, He took five loaves of bread and two fish from a young boy and shared it with the crowd. The food *never* ran out! There were even twelve basketfuls of broken pieces of bread left over.

—John 6:1-13

Another day, when Jesus was healing in a crowd of four thousand, plus women and children, He fed them all with only seven loaves of bread and a few fish. Again, there were left-overs.

—Matthew 15:29-38

When a tax collector questioned Peter about Jesus not paying taxes, Jesus easily solved the problem. He told Peter to go fishing and to open the mouth of the first fish he caught. Peter did as he was told and in the mouth of that fish was a coin. It was just the right amount to pay the taxes!

—Matthew 17:24-27

One day after talking to a crowd from one of Simon Peter's boats, Jesus told Peter to take Him out into the deep and let down the nets. Peter did just that even though he, James, and John had fished all night and had caught nothing. Well, this time they caught so many fish they had to get another boat to help pull the nets in!

—Luke 5:1-7

After Jesus was resurrected, He stood on the shore of the lake one morning watching the disciples fish. They were catching nothing. He yelled to tell them to put their nets on the right side of the boat. They did as they were told even though they didn't recognize Him. Of course, the nets were soon full. Then they knew who He was. Peter got so excited that he jumped out of the boat and swam to shore. Jesus had a fire ready and, right there on the beach, He prepared breakfast for those fishermen disciples.

—John 21:1-14

The Bible's most famous fishermen were Simon Peter and brother Andrew, James and John and their father Zebedee.

SPECIAL BIBLE NAMES AND NICKNAMES

Abraham	Father of Israel
	Friend of God
	Man of Faith
Barnabas	Son of Encouragement
Camel	Ship of the Desert
Canaan	The Promised Land
Comforter	The Holy Spirit
David	Sweet Singer of Israel
Disciples	Salt of the Earth
Herod Antipas	The Fox
James and John	Sons of Thunder
Jeremiah	The Weeping Prophet
John	The Baptist
John	Beloved Disciple
Joseph of Arimathea	The Secret Disciple
Judas	The Betrayer
Manasseh	The Mad
Micah	The Prophet of the Poor
Og	The Giant King
Paul	The First Missionary
Peter	The Rock
Rahab	The Harlot
Satan	Father of Lies
Simon	The Zealot
Solomon	The Wise King
Stephen	The First Christian Martyr
Thomas	The Doubting Disciple

SAY IT IN SIMILE

Many people, places and things in the Bible had special characteristics for which they are particularly remembered. Recalling some of these characteristics makes it fun and easy to create similes similar to the ones listed below. See if you agree with the authors about the ones they have chosen; then complete the list with some of your own.

Mad as Manasseh

Strong as Samson

Short as Zacchaeus

Stubborn as Jonah

Wise as Solomon

Jealous as Saul

Patient as Job

Boring as "the begats"

Horrid as Herod

Blind as Bartimaeus

Grim as Golgotha

Wicked as Jezebel

Odd as the ark

_____

_____

_____

_____

_____

SUPERSILLY SENTENCES TO SAY

Tantalizing Tongue Twisters

Aquila crafted Cornelius a quaint quilt.

Reposing Moses, hosing roses.

Will Noah mow a boa?

Righteous Ruth raises really ripe raisins.

Satan's sneaky snare snaps suddenly.

Job's lobes resting on robes.

Thick thistles and thorns
created Christ's cruel crown.

The fishermen four fillet fat fish with a flat fork.

Anxious Adam eyed the apple evil Eve ate.

Zacchaeus shimmied swiftly down
the Sycamore tree.

OBJECT - TIVITY

There are many interesting objects in the Scriptures, around which a story or event takes place. See if you can fill in each space with the name of a Bible character who goes with each object listed.

1. A sling _____
2. A cruse of oil _____
3. Five loaves and two fishes _____
4. A bowl of soup _____
5. A brass serpent _____
6. A scarlet rope _____
7. A sheet full of animals _____
8. A silver cup _____
9. A rod that becomes a serpent _____
10. A golden calf _____
11. A piece of forbidden fruit _____
12. A sundial _____
13. Jars and lanterns _____
14. A fleece _____
15. A woven basket _____
16. A head on a platter _____
17. A sea monster _____
18. A talking donkey _____
19. A great fish _____
20. Thirty pieces of silver _____
21. A pillar of salt _____
22. A crown of thorns _____
23. A sycamore tree _____
24. A burning bush _____
25. A coat of many colors _____

SOME VERY UNUSUAL MEALS...

- Joseph served his brothers a very unusual meal when they came to Egypt. Benjamin got five times as much as the others! *Genesis 43:31-34*

- Manna from the sky! *Exodus 16:35*

- Men ate the bread of angels, meat that "rained" down on them from heaven and quail swept in by the sea winds. Then they died! *Numbers 11:18-33 and Psalm 78: 23-31*

- On his way to find a wife, Samson discovered a very unusual snack in a very unusual place. *Judges 14:1-20*

- A coronation feast was stopped short when David anointed Solomon king. *1 Kings 1:32-35*

- Elijah was fed by ravens. *1 Kings 17:6*

- Elijah was fed cake, water and meat by an angel. *1 Kings 19:5-8*

- Two women agreed to boil their sons. They ate one, then the other one broke her promise and hid her son. *2 Kings 6:29*

- Bears mauled children who called Elisha "Baldy!" *2 Kings 2:23, 24*

- While preparing a community meal for some of the prophets, Elisha's servant made a mistake and put a poison vine into the stew. The man cried out and could not eat it. Elisha solved the problem by adding some flour to the pot. Then they all ate safely. *2 Kings 4:38-41*

- Elisha fed 100 hungry men with 20 loaves of barley bread and had plenty left over! *2 Kings 4:42-44*

- At Belshazzar's feast, a mysterious hand wrote on a wall. *Daniel 5*

- King Ahasuerus threw a lavish feast to show off the riches of his kingdom. *Esther 1:5-9*

- Jonah was a meal for a fish (but the fish got sick!) *Jonah 1, 2*

- Jesus and the disciples ate grain on the Sabbath. *Mark 2:23-28*

- Jesus fed 4,000 people with seven loaves and a few small fish and had seven basketfulls of broken pieces left over! *Matthew 15:32-39*

- Jesus went home to have dinner with a sinner named Zacchaeus, much to everyone's surprise. *Luke 19:1-10*

- Jesus ate with a whole group of tax collectors and sinners at Matthew's house and was criticized by the Pharisees. *Matthew 9:9-13*

- The last supper Jesus shared with his disciples before the Crucifixion was the scene of many unusual conversations and happenings. They all ate from one bowl! *Matthew 26:17-29*

- Jesus cooked breakfast for a group of tired disciples on the beach at Galilee. *John 21:1-12*

123

HOLY MOLY!

Each definition below should remind you of a pair of rhyming words.

1. Tags the first young brother put on his sheep.
2. Truths from the 5th book of the New Testament.
3. If Noah's boat had burned, there would have been lots of these!
4. Moses' adventuresome older brother.
5. A description of the Israelites' hunger for meat.
6. Weapons of the king's archers.
7. Cooking vessels belonging to Abraham's nephew.
8. Extra pounds put on by the world's first child.
9. Said of the citizens of a wicked twin city to Gomorah.
10. What leprechauns of Caesar's capitol might have been called.
11. A pagan God's cries.
12. A poetic song of peace.
13. Holes through which a famous Roman officer laced his shoes.
14. What someone probably said to Jesus' family when his mother died.
15. Could be said about the first father's sons.
16. Hugging serpents belonging to the captain of a famous ark.
17. What a loving young prophet's servants answered to his commands.
18. A title which might have been given to Samson after he brought the temple tumbling down.
19. When the early Christian churches had troubles, someone probably gave this cry for help.
20. What the Roman governor might have ordered his chief officer to do with Jesus' death certificate.
21. A famous Roman emperor's nose.

Note: *If you want to use this page as a game, cover the answers and try to guess. When you have learned the answers, try them on your friends!*

ANSWERS: 1. ABEL'S LABELS / 2. ACTS FACTS / 3. ARK'S SPARKS / 4. DARIN' AARON / 5. RAVEN CRAVIN' / 6. PHAROAH'S ARROWS / 7. LOT'S POTS / 8. CAIN'S GAINS / 9. SODOM GOT 'EM / 10. ROME'S GNOMES / 11. BAAL'S WAILS / 12. CALM PSALM / 13. PILATE'S EYELETS / 14. BURY MARY / 15. ADAM HAD 'EM / 16. NOAH'S BOAS / 17. OK HOSEA / 18. PILLAR KILLER / 19. CALL PAUL / 20. FILE IT, PILATE! / 21. CAESAR'S SNEEZER

124

NUMBER KNOWLEDGE

Fill in each space with the correct number!

A. _____ loaves and _____ fishes

B. _____ Hebrew boys in a furnace

C. _____ times around Jericho

D. _____ disciples

E. _____ lepers healed and _____ says, "Thank you."

F. _____ commandments given to Moses

G. _____ tribes of Israel

H. _____ pieces of silver to betray Jesus

I. _____ days and nights of rain

J. _____ plagues for the Egyptians

K. _____ times a day, Daniel prayed

L. _____ books in the Old Testament

M. _____ books in the New Testament

N. _____ members of the Godhead

O. _____ fed with a boy's lunch

P. _____ times Naaman dips in the River Jordan

Q. _____ books in the Bible

R. _____ days and nights in the belly of a whale

S. _____ sons of Jacob

T. _____ sons of Noah

U. _____ thieves crucified with Jesus

V. _____ days and nights from death to Resurrection

W. _____ spies hidden in Jericho by Rahab

X. _____ foolish virgins

Y. _____ wise virgins

Z. _____ true God

ANSWERS:

A. 5, 2 B. 3 C. 7 D. 12 E. 10, 1 F. 10 G. 12 H. 30 I. 40 J. 10 K. 3
L. 39 M. 27 N. 3 O. 5,000 P. 7 Q. 66 R. 3 S. 12 T. 3 U. 2 V. 3
W. 2 X. 5 Y. 5 Z. 1

READ ALL ABOUT IT!!!

A Reading List of Great Children's Books for Kids and Adults

A BIBLE DICTIONARY FOR YOUNG READERS by William N. McElrath, Broadman

BIBLE ENCYCLOPEDIA FOR CHILDREN by Dr. Cecil Northcott, Westminster Press

THE BIG BOOK OF BIBLE CRAFTS AND PROJECTS by Joy Mac-Kenzie, Zondervan/Impact (224 pages of exciting activities for all ages!)

THE BIG BOOK OF BIBLE GAMES AND PUZZLES by Shirley Bledsoe and Joy MacKenzie, Zondervan/Impact (Great for home, school, trips and long church services!)

THE BOOK OF LIFE by V. Gilbert Beers, Zondervan (The entire Bible in a dazzling, 24-volume "Childcraft/World Book" context. Magnificently created as a resource for personal Bible reading, devotions and problem-solving as well as a research tool for group Bible study, lesson and sermon preparation. Appropriate for young children, family groups and sophisticated clergy alike!)

CATHERINE MARSHALL'S STORY BIBLE by Catherine Marshall, Chosen/Crossroad (One of the most beautiful Bible story books ever... illustrated by children.)

THE CHILDREN'S ILLUSTRATED BIBLE DICTIONARY by Gilbert Beers, Thomas Nelson

THE CHURCH—LEARNING ABOUT GOD'S PEOPLE by Carole S. Matthews, Concordia (The church, defined clearly and beautifully!)

FAITH, HOPE AND LOVE—LEARNING ABOUT 1 CORINTHIANS 13 by Donald S. Roberts, Concordia (Clear, simple definitions of these words in children's language.)

GOD AND ME by Florence Parry Heide, Concordia (Junior and Grandpa can enjoy and learn from this together!)

IF I SHOULD DIE, IF I SHOULD LIVE by Joanne Marxhausen, Concordia (A beautiful explanation of death for the believer.)

IF YOU LIVED IN BIBLE TIMES by Nancy S. Williamson, Victor (Life in the first century—from a child's viewpoint.)

JESUS, MY FOREVER FRIEND by William Coleman, Chariot (An absolutely gorgeous introduction to life and culture during the time of Jesus' earthly ministry as well as an intriguing introduction to Jesus Christ, the person, and a unique approach to Christian principles, applied to everyday experience.)

A PICTURE BOOK OF JEWISH HOLIDAYS by David A. Adler, Holiday House

READ-ALOUD BIBLE STORIES—VOLUME I by Ella K. Lindvall, Moody Press (Six Bible stories for preschool/early grades, exquisitely written and illustrated in their language!)

THE TEN COMMANDMENTS—LEARNING ABOUT GOD'S LAW by Gloria A. Truitt, Concordia (The Ten Commandments translated for children, with stories of real-life application.)

3-IN-1—A PICTURE OF GOD by Joanne Marxhausen, Concordia (Finally, even adults can understand the Trinity!)

WHO, WHAT, WHEN, WHERE BOOK ABOUT THE BIBLE by William L. Coleman, Chariot (Possibly the most "fun" and most informative book about the Bible ever created for kids… guaranteed hours of enjoyment!)

THE WORLD INTO WHICH JESUS CAME by Sylvia Root Tester, Standard (A beautifully illustrated account of life in Bible times.)

WHO'S WHO???

AARON—Moses' older brother; first high priest of Israel

ABEDNEGO—Friend of Daniel, thrown into a furnace by Nebuchadnezzar

ABEL—Son of Adam and Eve; murdered by his brother, Cain

ABIGAIL—David's second wife

ABRAHAM—Father of the Hebrew nation; husband of Sarah; "friend of God"

ABRAM—Another name for Abraham

ABSALOM—Son of David

ACHAN—Thief stoned for looting at Jericho

ADAM—First man; husband of Eve; father of Cain, Abel and Seth

AHAB—A wicked king of Israel; husband of Jezebel

AHASUERUS—King of Persia; Esther's husband

AMOS—Old Testament prophet

ANANIAS—Early believer who lied to the Holy Spirit; struck dead with wife, Sapphira

ANDREW—Apostle; brother of Peter; fisherman

APOLLOS—Enthusiastic believer, taught by Aquila and Priscilla

ATHALIAH—Daughter of Jezebel; killed her grandsons to become queen

AUGUSTUS—Roman Emperor when Jesus was born

BAAL—Pagan god; his prophets had a "contest" with the prophet, Elijah

BALAAM—Prophet for Balak; his donkey saw an angel and spoke to him!

BARABBAS—Criminal released by Pilate in place of Jesus

BARAK—Judge of Israel

BARNABAS—Friend of Paul; joined Paul on his first missionary journey

BARTHOLOMEW—Apostle; also known as Nathanael; friend of Philip

BARTIMAEUS—Blind man healed by Jesus

BATH-SHEBA—Wife of Uriah and later, David; mother of Solomon

128

BELSHAZZAR—King of Babylon; handwriting on the wall occurred at one of his feasts. Daniel served him as interpreter.

BELTESHAZZAR—Daniel's Babylonian name

BOAZ—Husband of Ruth; great-grandfather of David

CAESAR—Emperor of Rome

CAIAPHAS—High priest of Israel who tried Jesus

CAIN—Son of Adam and Eve; murderer of his brother Abel

CALEB—Spy sent to Jericho with Joshua

CLEOPAS—He and a friend met Christ on the road to Emmaus after the Resurrection

CORNELIUS—Roman captain converted to Christianity by Paul; first Gentile convert

CYRUS—King of Persia

DAGON—Philistine god

DAN—Son of Jacob; brother of Joseph

DANIEL—Hebrew boy captive in Babylon; interpreter and prophet to kings; Old Testament author.

DARIUS—Babylonian king served by Daniel

DARIUS—Persian king served by Daniel

DAVID—Second king of Israel; boy warrior against Goliath; psalmist; son of Jesse; father of Solomon; wise ruler

DEBORAH—Wise judge of Israel; held court under a palm tree

DELILAH—Tricked Samson into telling her the secret of his strength

DINAH—Daughter of Jacob and Leah

DORCAS—Early Christian known for helping others; raised from the dead by Peter

ELEAZAR—Son of Aaron

ELI—High priest of Israel who trained Samuel

ELIJAH—Old Testament prophet under Ahab and Jezebel; went to heaven in a chariot of fire

ELISHA—Old Testament prophet who followed Elijah

ELISABETH—Mother of John the Baptist; wife of Zacharias

ENOCH—Was taken into heaven without dying, at age 365; Methuselah's father

ESAU—Son of Isaac; brother of Jacob

ESTHER—Beautiful Jewish girl who married King Ahashuerus and saved her people

EUNICE—Mother of Timothy

129

WHO'S WHO?

EUTYCHUS—Young believer who fell asleep during one of Paul's long sermons and fell from a window. Paul brought him back to life.

EVE—First woman; wife of Adam; mother of Cain, Abel and Seth

EZEKIEL—Old Testament prophet; taken captive into Babylon

EZRA—Leader of the Jews who were captive in Babylon; priest and scribe; led his people back to their homeland.

FELIX—Roman governor in Caesarea who kept Paul in prison

FESTUS—Successor of Felix who heard Paul's case and took him to Agrippa

GABRIEL—Angel who announced to Mary, Jesus' birth, and to Zacharias, the birth of John the Baptist

GAD—Son of Jacob; brother of Joseph

GAIUS—Companion of Paul

GIDEON—Israelite military leader and judge; set his fleece to test God's message to him; captured Midianite camp with jars, torches, horns and only 300 men!

GOLIATH—Philistine soldier killed by the boy David

GOMER—Beloved wife of Hosea; unfaithful

HABAKKUK—Old Testament prophet and author

HAGAR—Maid of Sarah; bore Abraham's son, Ishmael

HAGGAI—Old Testament prophet and author

HAM—Son of Noah

HAMAN—Wicked prime minister to Ahashuerus; his plot to kill the Jews was thwarted by Esther and Mordecai

HANNAH—Mother of Samuel

HEROD THE GREAT—King of Judea at birth of Christ; ordered all babies under 2 years old to be killed

HEROD ANTIPAS—Governor of Judea at Christ's Crucifixion; refused to hear Jesus' case; beheaded John the Baptist

HEROD AGRIPPA I—Governor of Judea; killed James, the brother of John; put Peter in prison; died of worms

HERODIAS—Wife of Herod Antipas; mother of Salome; plotted death of John the Baptist

HEZEKIAH—One of Judah's best kings; father of Manasseh, the Mad; prayed for Jerusalem, and the enemy was destroyed.

HOSEA—Old Testament prophet; husband of Gomer

ISAAC—Son of Abraham and Sarah; father of Jacob and Esau; husband of Rebekah

ISAIAH—Old Testament prophet who predicted Jesus' birth

ISHMAEL—Son of Abraham and Hagar

JACOB—Son of Isaac and Rebekah; husband of Rachel; brother of Esau; father of twelve sons, including Joseph

JAIRUS—Synagogue leader whose daughter Jesus raised from the dead

JAMES—Son of Zebedee; an apostle; brother of John

JAMES—Known as James the Greater; another apostle

JAMES—The brother of Jesus

JEHOSHAPHAT—King of Judah; smashed idols of Baal

JEHU—King of Judah; a wild chariot driver; killed Ahab

JEREMIAH—An Old Testament prophet who wept bitterly over the sins of his people

JEREBOAM—First king of Israel after the divided kingdom

JESSE—Father of David

JESUS CHRIST—Lord and Savior!

JEZEBEL—Wicked wife of King Ahab; mother of Athaliah; fell out a window and was eaten by dogs as Elijah had promised!

JOANNA—Early Christian convert by Paul

JOASH—Became king of Judah at age 7; surviving grandson of wicked grandmother, Athaliah!

JOB—Godly man who remained faithful to God in spite of terrible suffering

JOEL—Old Testament prophet

JOHN—Son of Zebedee; brother of James; an apostle

JOHN THE BAPTIST—First cousin of Jesus; baptized Jesus; beheaded by Herod Antipas

JONAH—Prophet who ran from God and was swallowed by a fish; repented and went to Nineveh to preach

JONATHAN—Son of Saul; good friend of David

WHO'S WHO?

JOSEPH—Son of Jacob; enslaved in Egypt

JOSEPH—Husband of Mary; foster-father of Jesus

JOSEPH OF ARIMATHEA—Secret disciple who buried Jesus in his private tomb

JOSEPH—Brother of Jesus

JOSHUA—Leader of Israel after Moses; conquered Jericho

JOSIAH—Became king of Judah at 8 years of age

JUDAH—Son of Jacob

JUDAS—One of the twelve apostles; also called Thaddaeus

JUDAS—Brother of Jesus

JUDAS ISCARIOT—One of the twelve apostles; betrayed Jesus for 30 pieces of silver

LABAN—Brother of Rebekah; father of Rachel and Leah

LAMECH—Father of Noah

LAZARUS—Friend of Jesus; brother of Mary and Martha; raised from the dead by Jesus

LEAH—Wife of Jacob

LEVI—A son of Jacob

LEVI—Another name for Matthew

LOIS—Grandmother of Timothy

LOT—Abraham's nephew; his wife turned to salt

LUKE—Companion of Paul; doctor; wrote the Gospel of Luke

LYDIA—Wealthy woman who became a Christian through Paul

MALACHI—Old Testament prophet and author

MANASSEH—Son of Joseph

MANASSEH—Mad King of Judah

MENOAH—Father of Samson

MARK—Companion of Paul; author of Mark's Gospel

MARTHA—Sister of Mary and Lazarus

MARY—Mother of Jesus

MARY—Sister of Martha and Lazarus

MARY MAGDALENE—A special friend of Jesus; first one to see the risen Christ

MATTHEW—Tax collector, turned apostle; author of Matthew's Gospel

MATTHIAS—Apostle who replaced Judas Iscariot

MEPHIBOSHETH—Son of Jonathan; lame

MESHACH—Hebrew friend of Daniel, thrown into furnace by Nebuchadnezzar

METHUSELAH—Son of Enoch; oldest man ever known to have lived; died at 969; grandfather of Noah

MICAH—Old Testament prophet and author

MICHAEL—A special angel

MICHAL—Daughter of Saul; wife of David

MIRIAM—Older sister of Moses and Aaron

MORDECAI—Cousin of Esther

MOSES—Leader of Israel's people during the Egyptian captivity and wilderness wanderings. God gave him the Ten Commandments.

NAAMAN—Syrian army commander who had leprosy; followed Elisha's orders to dip in the Jordan River seven times.

NABAL—Selfish first husband of Abigail

NABOTH—Stoned to death so Ahab and Jezebel could have his vineyard

NAHUM—Old Testament prophet and author

NAOMI—Mother-in-law and friend of Ruth

NAPHTALI—Son of Jacob

NATHAN—Prophet in David's time

NATHANIEL—Apostle; also called Bartholomew

NEBUCHADNEZZAR—Babylonian king whom Daniel served; known for fiery furnace and lions' den incidents

NEHEMIAH—Rebuilt the walls of Jerusalem after the Babylonian captivity; a man of prayer

NICODEMUS—Jewish leader who came to Jesus by night; claimed Jesus' body after the Crucifixion.

NOAH—Builder of the ark; father of Shem, Ham and Japheth

OBADIAH—Old Testament prophet and author

OBED—Father of Jesse; son of Ruth and Boaz

OG—A giant king who had a 14-foot-long bed

ONESIMUS—A runaway slave whom Paul begged Philemon to take back

PAUL—A Pharisee turned Christian; the first missionary; wrote many books of the New Testament

PETER—Andrew's fisherman brother; an apostle; New Testament author

PHILEMON—Early Christian leader; friend of Paul

PHILIP—An apostle; friend of Bartholomew

PHILIP—An evangelist

PILATE—Roman officer who tried Jesus

POTIPHAR—Pharoah's captain whose wife tried to seduce Joseph

PRISCILLA—Wife of Aquila; friend of Paul

QUIRINIUS—Governor of Syria at time of Jesus' birth

RACHEL—Wife of Jacob; mother of Joseph and Benjamin

RAHAB—Prostitute in Jericho who hid the spies, Caleb and Joshua

REBEKAH—Wife of Isaac; mother of Esau and Jacob

REHEBOAM—First king of Judah

REUBEN—Oldest son of Jacob

RHODA—Early believer in Jerusalem; left Peter standing knocking at the gate.

RUTH—Great-grandmother of David; wife of Boaz; friend and daughter-in-law to Naomi

SALOME—Daughter of Herodias; plotted with her mother to behead John the Baptist

SAMSON—Judge of Israel; betrayed by Delilah

SAMUEL—Prophet and judge, trained in the temple by Eli; anointed Saul and David as kings

SAPPHIRA—Wife of Ananias with whom she plotted to lie against the Holy Spirit; died for her deed

SARAH—Wife of Abraham; mother of Isaac

SATAN—The Devil; God's enemy

SAUL—The first king of United Israel

SAUL—Another name for Paul

SETH—Son of Adam and Eve; brother of Cain and Abel

SHADRACH—Hebrew friend of Daniel, thrown into the furnace by Nebuchadnezzar

SHEM—Son of Noah

SILAS—Friend of Paul; missionary

SIMEON—Son of Jacob

SIMON—Another name for Peter

SIMON—Brother of Jesus

SIMON—The leper

SIMON—The tanner

SIMON—The magician

SIMON OF CYRENE—Early Christian who carried Jesus' cross

SIMON THE ZEALOT—An apostle

SOLOMON—Son of David; third king of United Israel; wrote Proverbs, Ecclesiastes, and Song of Solomon

STEPHEN—Stoned as the first Christian martyr

TABITHA—Another name for Dorcas

TERAH—Father of Abraham

THADDAEUS—An apostle; also called Judas

THOMAS—An apostle; put his hands in Jesus' nail-prints to be sure it was He

TIBERIUS—Emperor at the time of Jesus' Crucifixion

TIMOTHY—Friend of Paul

TITUS—Friend of Paul

URIAH—First husband of Bath-Sheba; sent into battle by David to be killed

UZZAH—Touched the ark of the covenant to steady it and was struck dead

VASHTI—Queen of Persia before Esther

ZACHARIAS—Father of John the Baptist; husband of Elisabeth

ZACCHAEUS—Short tax collector who climbed a tree to see Jesus

ZECHARIAH—Old Testament prophet and author

ZEBULUN—Son of Jacob

ZEDEKIAH—Last king of Judah

ZIPPORAH—Wife of Moses

WHO'S WHO?

RUMPERSTICKERS
On The End of Whose Camel Would You Find…??

DON'T KNOCK ROCK

GOIN' TO THE DOGS

SEE MORE FROM A SYCAMORE

HELP WANTED: HEXPERIENCE NECESSARY

BEWARE OF FALLEN ARCHES

ANSWERS:

Peter, Jezebel, Zacchaeus, Satan, Samson

Does your Mark-A-MAP look like this one? (p.103)

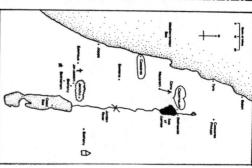

MY OWN LISTS